FROM BLOODY SHIRT
TO FULL DINNER PAIL

FROM BLOODY SHIRT TO FULL DINNER PAIL

The Transformation of Politics and Governance in the Gilded Age

CHARLES W. CALHOUN

Hill and Wang

A division of Farrar, Straus and Giroux

New York

Hill and Wang
A division of Farrar, Straus and Giroux
18 West 18th Street, New York 10011

Library of Congress Cataloging-in-Publication Data
Calhoun, Charles W. (Charles William), 1948–
    From bloody shirt to full dinner pail : the transformation of politics and
governance in the Gilded Age / Charles W. Calhoun.— 1st ed.
        p.   cm.
    Includes bibliographical references and index.
    ISBN 978-0-8090-4793-2 (hardcover : alk. paper)
    1. United States—Politics and government—1865–1900.   I. Title.

E661 .C225   2010
973.8—dc22

                                                        2010002429

Designed by Jonathan D. Lippincott

www.fsgbooks.com

1   3   5   7   9   10   8   6   4   2

To
Liz Calhoun
and her friends

Contents

Preface

If the first decade of the twenty-first century has shown us anything, it is the momentous influence of national politics and public policy, not only in the life of the nation but also in the lives of individuals. The national elections in this period have made abundantly clear that what politicians do and what voters decide can have huge consequences. One need go no further than to compare the actual record of the George W. Bush administration with an imagined record of an Al Gore presidency to recognize that the victory of one party and the defeat of another do much to determine the course of the nation. This has been true throughout American history, although the sharpness in the changes of direction has varied from one era to another.

Over the past thirty or forty years, many, perhaps most, professional historians have followed their interests into areas outside the political realm. Social history, cultural history, and other new emphases in the exploration of the past have ventured into uncharted territory and thus have broadened our understanding of America's development. Yet, enlightening as these new approaches may be, they cannot mask the truth that politics defines and permeates our national culture. The impact of politics is inescapable in a republic marked by frequent elections that determine who shall hold the reins of power. Through government and the politics that shape it, Americans have sought to modulate differences, resolve problems, and chart their collective destiny.

In no other era in American history has citizen interest in politics and governance been more intense than during the late nineteenth century, the period known as the Gilded Age. In presidential elections, voter turnout typically surpassed 75 percent, and in some states it exceeded 90 percent. Partisan feeling ran high, and despite the fleeting appeal of third parties, most citizens fervently identified with either the Republican or the Democratic Party. As the rising young politician Theodore Roosevelt put it, "Every man who wishes well to his country is in honor bound to take an active part in political life."[1]

Sandwiched between the age of sectionalism and the Civil War on the one hand and the Progressive Era on the other, the politics of the Gilded Age can seem inconsequential. In reality, however, Americans who lived during this era, politicians and citizens alike, saw matters of great significance at stake. The period witnessed a profound transformation—from a near fixation on questions relating to race and section to a new focus on economic matters. In the parlance of the day, political attention turned from "sentimental" issues to "practical" ones that addressed the material condition of the nation and its people. The American polity moved from waving the bloody shirt to arguing over the best way to keep the average American's dinner pail full. This book presents in brief compass how this transformation unfolded and how it put Americans' pocketbook concerns at the top of the political agenda, where they have remained ever since.

I have devoted my entire professional career to examining the political life and culture of the late nineteenth century, and what I have written here represents a concise take on a complicated era. In my research over the years, I have accumulated a host of debts. I am grateful for the splendid assistance of numerous librarians, most notably the staff of the Library of Congress's Manuscript Reading Room, led by the indefatigable Jeff Flannery. I have been fortunate to receive support for my work from a number of sources, and I particularly express my gratitude to the National Endowment for the Humanities for a fellowship and the Thomas Harriot College of Arts and Sciences of East Carolina University for a College Research Award.

Lewis L. Gould and R. Hal Williams have been more than generous in sharing their findings and insights with me and in numerous other ways. I have also benefited from the work and observations, both formal and informal, of my fellow laborers in the Gilded Age vineyards, including Michael Les Benedict, Roger Bridges, Ed Crapol, Michael Holt, Ari Hoogenboom, Wayne Morgan, Allan Peskin, Brooks Simpson, and Mark Summers. Of course, I alone am responsible for what I have written.

I am grateful for the interest in this project shown by Thomas LeBien, publisher at Hill and Wang, and I thank editor Dan Crissman for his careful and thoughtful reading of the manuscript.

I deeply appreciate the encouragement of my colleagues in the East Carolina University history department, especially its chair, Gerry Prokopowicz, for arranging my teaching schedule to expedite the preparation of this work and for the many other manifestations of his support. The department's capable staff, Rebecca Futrell, Barbara Utz, and Katrina Person, have facilitated my work in countless ways.

Finally, as always, I owe my greatest debt to my family: my sisters, Judy Blakely and Mary Howard, who form a wonderful cheering section from afar; my wife, Bonnie, whose love and patience sustain me; and my dear daughter, Elizabeth, to whom I dedicate this book with love.

Charles W. Calhoun

FROM BLOODY SHIRT
TO FULL DINNER PAIL

Introduction

At the onset of the Gilded Age, the American political universe exhibited a paradoxical blend of stability and disarray. The pattern of two-party rivalry had existed since George Washington's day, so partisan structures and methods were well established. Yet for more than two decades the system had suffered profound turmoil. Slavery, especially the question of its expansion, and the intense sectional hostility it fueled lay at the root of the upheaval. In 1861, after seventy years under the Constitution, the system at last experienced a colossal breakdown when rebels in a third of the states sought to abandon the Union rather than accept the legitimate results of a presidential election. For four years the federal government was forced to wage war to maintain not only the country's geographic integrity but also the viability of its republican polity—what President Abraham Lincoln described as "government of the people, by the people, for the people."

Yet even during this, the nation's darkest hour, the competitive two-party system retained its essential vigor, at least in the loyal section of the country. Despite some government abridgment of civil liberties and the absence of the South from electoral contention, an opposition party—the Democrats—showed remarkable vitality, garnering 45 percent of the popular vote in the sole wartime presidential election, in 1864. The institutional tumult continued into the post-war years. The Republican Congress fought with President Andrew Johnson over fundamental questions of how best to reconstruct the nation: How could "seceded" states regain their correct relationship with the federal union? Who (former Confederates? former slaves?) would have the right to vote? How could the sanctity of the ballot be guaranteed? Again, however, the unsettled nature of the polity did not slow the resurgence of two-party contention. In 1868 Democrat Horatio Seymour amassed 47 percent of the popular vote against Union military hero Ulysses S. Grant, and six years later the Democrats won a commanding control of the national House of Representatives with 58 percent of the seats. From the 1870s to the 1890s American politics witnessed an intense struggle for supremacy between two mature, robust, evenly matched national parties.

This relentless battle for power is the subject of this book. Throughout the period, the Republican and Democratic parties remained the principal contenders, but the issues and principles over which they fought underwent a fundamental transformation. In 1868, in the first presidential election after the Civil War, matters of sectionalism, Reconstruction, and race still dominated political discourse. Twenty-eight years later, Republican William McKinley and Democrat William Jennings Bryan paid scant attention to such issues and concentrated their campaigns for the White House almost entirely on economic concerns.

The new focus was hardly unprecedented or the shift abrupt. Before the prolonged sectional crisis, Federalists had fought Republicans and Whigs had fought Democrats over taxation, internal improvements, and the Bank of the United States. For years before 1896, economic issues such as the tariff and the currency had achieved resurgent importance, gaining the attention of both politicians and voters. Indeed, in 1869 Grant devoted half of his first inaugural address to financial questions. During the Civil War, the federal government had wrought a complete overhaul of the nation's financial system, including vast increases in tariffs and internal taxes, the creation of note-issuing national banks, the issuing of the green-back currency unbacked by specie, and the accumulation of a huge national debt. How to accommodate this new structure to the demands of the postwar economy became a central question in American politics. And the need for such accommodation took on added urgency with the changing nature of the economy itself, especially its burgeoning industrialization, development of an extensive and complex transportation system, and maturation of national and international market structures.

Nonetheless, despite the growing salience of issues related to the government's role in the economy, matters of section and race remained conspicuous for years. Democrats brazenly accused Republicans of "waving the bloody shirt," but in the South, white Democrats who came to dominate the region's politics practiced a far more virulent sectionalist rhetoric, inflaming the emotions of the war and Reconstruction for partisan purposes well into the twentieth century. During the Gilded Age, northern Democrats generally acquiesced in this politics of malice, while Republicans had far more trouble maintaining a united front on the southern question. Many continued to espouse the higher aspirations of Reconstruction and felt genuine dismay over their inability to effect real change in the South. But in Republican Party councils, a persistent solicitude for the rights of blacks dueled with a push to shift to economic questions as the dominant concerns of Americans both north and south. By the mid-1890s the economic emphasis prevailed.

In retrospect, the general policy orientations of the two major parties in the Gilded Age seem in many ways the opposite of those of their counterparts a century later. Republicans of the late nineteenth century were much more the party of energy and activism, while the Democrats leaned toward laissez-faire. In addition, Democrats clung to a states' rights orthodoxy rooted in their party's Jeffersonian origins. The Republicans, in contrast, favored a strong and useful national government, one that especially implemented policies such as the protective tariff to foster economic growth. Democrats decried such policies as corrupt perversions of power in the service of special interests. Through much of the period, both parties suffered divisions over the currency question, but while the Republicans grew increasingly unified behind "sound" money, a trend culminating in McKinley's embrace of the gold standard in 1896, the Democrats' wrangles over monetary policy grew more heated and nearly tore the party apart in the 1890s. The basic policy orientations of the two major parties—Republicans' espousal of activist government and the Democrats' embrace of laissez-faire— were deeply rooted in the nineteenth century and would not undergo a fundamental reversal until after 1900.

Although both major parties shifted their focus toward economic issues, deep emotional scars endured, and the partition of the national electorate along sectional lines showed a remarkable persistence. With the demise of Reconstruction, Democrats secured a hammerlock on the South in the late 1870s, and from that time until 1920 not a single electoral vote from any state of the old Confederacy went to a Republican presidential candidate. Counterbalancing the Solid South, states in the Northeast, the upper Midwest, and the West formed a bloc slightly larger and nearly as reliable for the Republicans. But neither of these two blocs held enough electoral votes to win a presidential election. Victory usually depended on securing sufficient support in a handful of so-called doubtful states. The most important swing states were New York and Indiana, rich in electoral votes, with Connecticut and New Jersey playing lesser roles. The electorate in these states was so evenly divided that one could rarely predict which way they would go. Between 1872 and 1896, neither New York nor Indiana voted for the presidential nominee of the same party in two successive elections. In presidential election years, the parties focused their attention on these states: assigning their best speakers, spending the greater part of their campaign

funds, and working hardest to perfect their organization. Democrats
and Republicans often looked to these states for national nominees.
Between 1876 and 1892 the two parties made twenty nominations
for president and vice president; thirteen went to men from New
York or Indiana. In addition, the doubtful states offered the likeliest
fields where vote buying or other underhanded schemes could influence the outcome.

The equilibrium between Republicans and Democrats in the
nationwide electorate often contributed to divided government in Washington. After 1874, rarely did the same party control both houses of
Congress plus the presidency. Congress itself was often split, the
Democrats usually holding a majority in the House of Representatives while the Republicans controlled the Senate. These divisions
put a premium on cooperation across the aisle, a rarity in the Gilded
Age, when partisanship ran high. Obstructionism, particularly by
the Democrats, put limits on action and thus helped to give governance in the period a reputation for ineffectuality and indifference.

Moreover, disunity within the parties could further impede effectiveness. Competition among leaders for prominence and power
sometimes degenerated into bitter rivalry and spawned long-term
factional animosities. Such internal strife might grow out of personal
clashes or ideological differences or both. Often factional antagonism was manifested in the competition for patronage, the tussle
over which set of leaders would have the power to place their allies
in office. At the national level, the spoils system constituted the personnel recruitment program for the federal bureaucracy, which in
the Gilded Age surpassed 150,000 positions. The Pendleton Civil
Service Act of 1883 moderated the patronage struggle to some degree and provided a modicum of relief to leaders who bridled at the
onerous task of finding jobs for party cadres.

Ideological disenchantment occasionally led some Americans
to abandon the Democrats and the Republicans altogether and to
turn instead to third parties. Groups such as the Greenbackers, the

Prohibitionists, and various labor parties often focused on a single issue or a small set of issues. None of them had a remote chance of achieving national power, although in the 1890s the Populists enjoyed substantial support in some states in the South and the West. Third parties were not without influence. Their vociferous advocacy of certain views occasionally moved the major parties to adopt similar stands. In addition, defections to third parties played havoc with the calculations of major party leaders in the doubtful states, where the loss of just a few votes could spell defeat in elections. In spite of their dim prospects for power, third parties exacerbated the volatility of Gilded Age politics.

Even so, most voters remained steadfastly loyal to one of the two major parties in local, state, and national elections. In presidential years, turnout averaged nearly 78 percent, far more than in any subsequent period. Moreover, for great numbers of citizens, political participation went beyond merely showing up at the polls. Political clubs attracted enthusiastic members across the nation, not only in cities but in small towns and rural areas as well. The parties themselves boasted open and broad-based organizations that invited participation in ward, precinct, town, city, and county committees. These groups looked upward in a pyramidal structure of district, state, and national committees. At each level, a party convention brought citizen activists together to select nominees and define party goals. Local issues and the local organization remained important to voters, but the party's quadrennial national nominating convention and the following presidential campaign operated as powerful forces for the renewal of partisan identification.

Historians and others have often dismissed the Gilded Age as a time when politics offered little more than corruption, empty rhetoric, and meaningless histrionics, when the Democrats and the Republicans stood alike as Tweedledum and Tweedledee and politicians fought merely for the spoils. In reality, Americans of the late nineteenth century took politics seriously, saw fundamental differences between the parties, and considered the matters at issue of vital importance. In the Gilded Age, if politics was blood sport, it was so because politics was in most people's blood. A great many citizens were convinced that the fate of the nation, as well as their own personal prospects, turned inexorably on the fortunes of their party.

In the early part of the period, contention focused on the very character of the nation and the polity. The Republicans sought to secure the results of the Civil War beyond a mere reunification of the country, and they strove to bring about a fundamental reordering of society in the South. Democrats and white southerners fought that effort tooth and nail for more than a decade, and it eventually failed. But even though sectional issues receded, Republicans did not surrender their national orientation. Instead, they set about framing a national economic program of tariff protection, a stable currency, and aid to business aimed at feeding a material development that would benefit the whole nation and its citizens. Democrats, in contrast, doubted that government-generated bounty would be equitably shared. They attacked government activism and cast themselves as the party of the people.

Citizens attended this conflict with intense interest and saw their own well-being at stake. As one party leader put it, the real battleground in politics became "the private home where each family began to examine and discuss for itself the policy of the parties to find which party promised the most for the elevation and comfort of that special home."[1] Seen in this light, political contention was no mere issueless scramble for office, but instead a relentless struggle for the hearts and minds of voters, with the policy direction of the nation hanging on the outcome. Ultimately, the struggle for supremacy between two governing ideals, not corruption and ballyhoo, marked the real significance of politics in the Gilded Age.

ONE

General in the White House

In 1868 Americans cast their ballots in the first presidential election since the end of the Civil War. To no one's surprise, issues related to the conflict and its aftermath, Reconstruction, cast a long shadow over the election campaign and its outcome. As its candidate for president, the Republican Party chose General Ulysses S. Grant, who had led the Union armies to victory in the spring of 1865.

A graduate of West Point, Grant had served capably as a junior officer during the Mexican War, demonstrating the resourcefulness and determination that marked him as a military leader to be reckoned with. Stationed at West Coast outposts during the early 1850s, however, he grew lonely and bored with peacetime service and resigned his commission in 1854. For the next seven years he struggled to support his family as he drifted from job to job, and 1861 found him clerking in his father's leather goods store in Illinois. The outbreak of the southern rebellion that year rescued him from obscurity. He returned to the army, and by early 1862 a series of victories in the western theater launched his rise in the Union army. His superiors soon recognized the depth of his strategic and tactical insight, his judgment regarding men, and his steady, unrelenting determination to achieve his and the nation's objectives. He had a clear understanding of the political questions at stake in the war and enjoyed good relations with most of his superiors, especially President Abraham Lincoln, but he showed little propensity for self-puffery. Unruffled by fame and taciturn almost to a fault, he allowed his deeds to speak for him. Three years into the war, Grant had risen to lieutenant general, a rank last held by George Washington, and he commanded all the Union armies.

Even before the Confederate surrender at Appomattox, many Republicans had concluded that Grant was the ideal candidate to lead the party's hosts in 1868. Initially the general did little to encourage the movement. After Appomattox he remained at the head of the army as general in chief, a position that could easily satisfy a soldier's appetite for honor and usefulness. He showed scant interest in a political career, and as a military man, he properly forbore commenting publicly on political issues.

Yet when the fight over how best to reconstruct the formerly seceded states grew more intense between the Republican Congress and the Democratic-leaning president, Andrew Johnson, and especially after Congress adopted military reconstruction in the South, Grant found himself inexorably drawn into the political vortex. He supported black suffrage as a key element in the remaking of the South, but his relative silence led some Radical Republicans to favor alternative presidential candidates more clearly identified with the cause. In 1867, however, when Republicans put the issue at the forefront of their campaigns in several northern state elections, they met a sharp rebuff from voters, an outcome that convinced most GOP leaders that Grant's nomination was indispensable to unite the party for the struggle in 1868. Moreover, Grant grew increasingly angry at Johnson's attempts to exploit him in his battles with Congress. Especially irksome was the president's dragging Grant into his attempt to dismiss Secretary of War Edwin Stanton in violation of the Tenure of Office Act, which in early 1868 led to Johnson's impeachment and near conviction. After three years of turmoil in Washington and mayhem in the South, Grant came to believe that the substantive consequences of the Union victory beyond the mere defeat of the Confederacy were in danger of being lost. "I could not back down," he wrote to his friend General William T. Sherman, without "leaving the contest for power for the next four years between mere trading politicians, the elevation of whom, no matter which party won, would lose to us, largely, the results of the costly war which we have gone through."[1]

Meeting in Chicago in May on the heels of Johnson's Senate acquittal, the Republican National Convention nominated Grant for president and House Speaker Schuyler Colfax for vice president. The platform condemned Johnson for treachery and usurpation and congratulated the country on the adoption of Congress's plan of reconstruction. The party upheld the granting of suffrage to black males in the South but asserted that the loyal northern states should determine the suffrage question for themselves. According to Maine Republican James G. Blaine, the hypocrisy of this "evasive and discreditable" position made party leaders "heartily ashamed of it long before the political canvass had closed." At the next session of Congress, Republicans passed the Fifteenth Amendment, outlawing racial discrimination in suffrage throughout the nation.[2]

The Republican platform also highlighted financial issues, especially the pressing question of the huge national debt left from the Civil War. During the conflict, the federal government had issued bonds totaling more than $2 billion, and by 1868 only a small portion had been repaid. The government had also issued more than $400 million in legal tender notes— the greenbacks—unbacked by specie. After the war, most Americans favored a resumption of specie payments—that is, the redemption of the greenbacks in coin. But because the greenbacks were a depreciated currency, not equivalent in value to gold and silver dollars, the question remained as to how to raise them up to parity with specie so that resumption could proceed without a drain on the government's gold supply.

In 1866 the Treasury Department had begun to withdraw greenbacks as a way to enhance the value of those remaining in circulation, but a severe business recession, caused largely by incidents and forces abroad, led Congress to halt the contraction in early 1868. As economic conditions worsened, many of the sufferers, especially in the agrarian West, drew comparisons between their own distress and the comfortable condition of well-to-do government bondholders, mostly in the East, who drew interest in gold on their tax-exempt bonds. In response, a movement associated most closely with Ohio Democrat George H. Pendleton called for the Treasury to pay the principal of a portion of the bonds in greenbacks in cases where the law did not specify repayment in gold. Although some Republicans flirted with this so-called Ohio Idea, the party's national platform in 1868 declared that "national honor" required that the government pay its creditors "not only according to the letter, but the spirit of the laws," that is, in gold. It denounced "all forms of repudiation as a national crime."[3]

As a member of Congress, Pendleton had opposed most of the Lincoln administration's war measures, including the issuance of the greenbacks. Now out of office and hoping to revive his political career by appealing to agrarian unrest, he switched sides on the money question. He had received the Democratic vice presidential nomination four years earlier, and he hoped to ride his economic program to the top spot in 1868. But Pendleton found little favor in the party's eastern hard-money wing and faced a crowded field of men, including Andrew Johnson, who aspired to take on Grant. At the national convention in New York, the platform endorsed the Ohio Idea, but its opponents stood firmly against the nomination of Pendleton, and the Democrats' requirement of a two-thirds vote prolonged the contest through twenty-two ballots. The ordeal ended in the selection of a dark horse, former New York governor Horatio Seymour.

A hard-money man, Seymour won few friends in the West on the currency issue, but he had great appeal for both eastern and western Democrats who wished to make denunciation of Republican Reconstruction policy the centerpiece of their campaign. A critic of the

Lincoln administration, Seymour had in 1863 addressed a New York City mob of murderous antidraft rioters as "my friends." He had supported Johnson in his battles with Congress and had attacked the Republicans for "cursing the people of the South with military despotism and negro domination." The Democrats' platform condemned the Reconstruction Acts as "unconstitutional, revolutionary, and void." Vice presidential nominee Frank Blair of Missouri, a former Union general who had recoiled at Radical Reconstruction, called for a Democratic administration to oust Republican officials in the South and "allow the white people to reorganize their own governments." Blair made a series of campaign speeches filled with raw racist invective, labeling blacks "a semi-barbarous race" determined to "subject the white women to their unbridled lust."[4]

Republicans eagerly picked up the gauntlet the Democrats had thrown down. GOP speakers and editors arraigned the Democrats for clinging to the spirit of the southern rebellion and warned that Blair's extremist views could incite a new civil war or a war of extermination against Republicans in the South. Never a comfortable public speaker, Grant kept quiet and monitored the campaign from his home in Galena, Illinois. In his brief public letter accepting nomination, he took the high road, promising to work for "peace, quiet and protection every where," and closing with the compelling epigram, "Let us have peace."[5] Seymour also stayed home, until heavy Democratic losses in state elections in September and October impelled him to take to the stump. In several speeches the Democratic nominee sought to divert attention to economic issues, alleging that Republican policies worked injury to average Americans and the nation at large. He denied any intention to undermine the results of the war.

Even so, violent outbreaks in the South tended to substantiate Republican charges. Especially in Georgia and Louisiana, the Ku Klux Klan and similar groups resorted to murder and other forms of intimidation to curb voting by blacks and their white Republican allies. These tactics proved effective. Seymour won those two states, and elsewhere in the South, Republican totals declined from previous levels.

In the nation at large, however, Grant carried the election with 214 electoral votes to 80 for Seymour. In the popular balloting, Grant's nationwide margin was much narrower. He won 52.7 percent of the vote, while Seymour garnered 47.3 percent. Although the Republicans retained lopsided control of Congress, the presidential popular vote showed that the two-party system had made a robust recovery from the war years. Even with a relatively weak candidate, the Democrats had managed a more than respectable showing against the savior of the Union.

Equally important was the apparent impact of the black vote. Grant won 300,000 more votes than Seymour, yet the African American vote was estimated at 500,000. With the help of black voters, Grant won six of the eight former Confederate states that participated in the election. In New York, where blacks had to meet a property qualification to vote, Seymour won by a margin of just 10,000 votes, less than 1.2 percent. Had that restriction not existed, Grant might well have won the state.

The precarious state of black voting in the South, as evinced in Georgia and Louisiana, coupled with its potential advantage to Republicans in the North, moved Republicans in the House and Senate to pass the Fifteenth Amendment even before Grant and the new Congress took office. They well knew that black suffrage rights nationwide would inure to their political benefit, but they also believed that, in the words of Ohio Radical Samuel Shellabarger, "The decisive argument for the amendment is that it is right."[6] After considerable debate, the legislators settled on a fairly conservative wording, banning discrimination in voting on the basis of race, color, or previous condition of servitude. This left the door open for other forms of discrimination (which southern states would adopt at the end of the century), but the majority of congressional Republicans concluded that, given the state of the public mind on the issue in 1868, this was the most that state legislatures would approve.

In March 1869 Grant entered upon his duties as president with a huge storehouse of goodwill. With the general's military achievements clear to all, his anticipated assets as a civilian leader had taken on towering proportions. Not the least of his virtues was that, like George Washington, he appeared to stand above petty partisan wrangling. Ohio senator John Sherman, the general's brother, assured Grant that the people regarded him as "so independent of party politics as to be a guarantee of Peace and quiet." Grant himself, initially at least, cultivated this image of Olympian detachment. Careful to differentiate himself from the overbearing Andrew Johnson, he promised that he would "on all subjects, have a policy to recommend, but none to enforce against the will of the people." "The office has come to me unsought," he told the nation in his inaugural address. "I commence its duties untrammeled." Deeply suspicious of politicians as a class, Grant did not yet fully appreciate that for a president to succeed as a tribune of the people, he must also be an effective leader of his party.[7]

In preparing his address, Grant refrained from asking the advice of Republican chieftains, thereby forgoing a courtesy that could have helped grease the wheels for his entry into his new associations in Washington. Even so, few Republicans could object to the doctrines he set forth. He devoted more than half of the speech to financial questions, calling for a safe return to specie payments and the payment of the national debt in gold unless the contract stipulated otherwise. On Reconstruction issues, he pledged to uphold the "security of person, property, and free religious and political opinion in every part of our common country, without regard to local prejudice." He urged the speedy ratification of the Fifteenth Amendment.[8]

Grant's drive to strike an independent course showed again in his cabinet selections. Showered with recommendations and unsolicited advice, he kept his own counsel and delayed announcing his

Ulysses S. Grant, eighteenth president of the United States (Library of Congress)

choices until the last minute. Fuller consultation with party leaders might have averted embarrassing missteps. Among those who aspired to be secretary of state was Massachusetts senator Charles Sumner, a prominent abolitionist before the war and the foremost leader of Radical Republicans during and after the conflict. A man of great erudition and commensurate arrogance, Sumner believed that his long service to the Republican Party, his wide foreign acquaintance, and his eight years as chairman of the Senate Foreign Relations Committee entitled him to head the State Department. But Sumner had never shown much enthusiasm about Grant's becoming president, and Grant, like many other men, considered the senator's blinding self-regard insufferable. Grant never seriously thought of appointing Sumner, and despite the president's efforts to conciliate him, Sumner's wounded pride never recovered. Instead, Grant gave the State Department to his patron in Illinois politics, Congressman Elihu Washburne, although Washburne served as secretary for only a week before resigning to become minister to France. To replace Washburne, Grant turned to Hamilton Fish, a former New York governor of ability and impeccable reputation.

For Treasury secretary, the president-elect had early determined to appoint Alexander T. Stewart, a New York merchant whose business acumen, at least as attested by his immense wealth, Grant greatly admired. Although Stewart won unanimous confirmation in the Senate, some Republicans disliked his low-tariff views, and the objection soon arose that his connection with commerce posed a legal bar to his taking the Treasury position. Sumner led the charge against Stewart, and the president reluctantly backed down. Grant next appointed Massachusetts congressman George S. Boutwell, a Sumner ally. He gave the War Department to his longtime military aide John A. Rawlins, and for secretary of the navy he chose the wealthy Philadelphia banker Adolph E. Borie, who exhibited little taste for the job and less capacity. The three other seats at the cabinet table went to Jacob D. Cox (Interior), John A. J. Creswell (postmaster general), and Ebenezer R. Hoar (attorney general), all eminently capable administrators. The cabinet secretaries varied widely in ability, but none could boast a substantial base from which to add political strength to the administration. Grant's manner of selection, moreover, seemed to belie the reputation he had earned as a general for shrewdness in choosing subordinates.

As Grant turned to the task of filling subordinate offices, he sought to throw off the shackles of the Tenure of Office Act, which barred the president from removing an appointee without Senate approval of a successor. Grant had hoped that before he took office, Congress would rescind this law, passed to restrain Johnson, but the Senate, again led by Sumner, refused to accept repeal. Once in the White House, Grant let office-hungry Republicans know that he would not begin a wholesale removal of Johnson appointees until the law was repealed. Nonetheless, jealous of its new (and unconstitutional) prerogative, the Senate balked. In the end, although outright repeal failed, Grant's allies in Congress secured passage of a compromise that in essence freed the president's hands in the matter of appointments.

This imbroglio with Congress notwithstanding, Grant made it clear that he and his department heads would follow the established practice of considering the advice of party congressmen and senators in making appointments. This decision to follow traditional patronage practices was less a rejection of independence than a candid recognition of reality. The federal bureaucracy had grown to tens of thousands of positions, and it was physically impossible for Grant and the cabinet secretaries to handle the appointments unassisted. Whatever its political uses and susceptibility to abuse, the practice of congressional patronage had emerged as a logical, if cumbersome, component of the federal personnel system, which Grant was willing to continue. But to the reform-minded, especially those who had expected to wield influence in the new administration but did not, Grant's course seemed both a betrayal and a surrender to machine politicians. Within weeks Henry Adams was complaining that the new administration was "far inferior to the last" and that in the matter of appointments, his friends had "almost all lost ground instead of gaining it as I hoped."[9] The civil service reform movement had originated in opposition to Johnson's policies, but Grant's course gave the movement a new impetus for years to come. Moreover, Grant's presumption in ignoring Adams and other elite opinion makers ensured that his policy would suffer a searing criticism, tainting not only his image among his contemporaries but his place in history as well.

Many of these critics found more to like, initially at least, in Grant's monetary policy. They hailed his inaugural pledges to uphold the nation's honor by paying its debts in gold and moving toward specie payments. They were equally pleased two weeks later when these principles were embodied in the first law Grant signed, the Public Credit Act. But Grant and Treasury secretary George Boutwell could not launch specie payments immediately, because the premium on gold was still about 30 percent; that is, on the open market it took $130 in greenbacks to acquire $100 in gold. Although hard-money advocates favored contraction of the greenbacks to raise their value and reduce the premium, such a course remained politically unfeasible. Hence, Grant and Boutwell adopted a conservative policy of "growing up" to specie resumption, which would follow naturally from economic expansion. They believed that as the nation's business increased, so too would the need for sufficient currency to carry it on. Of necessity, the greenbacks would grow in public use, their value would rise, and they would eventually reach par with gold, at which point the Treasury could safely offer specie in exchange.

The administration was scarcely six months old when this policy experienced a brush with disaster. In a scheme known to history as the New York Gold Conspiracy, notorious speculators Jay Gould and Jim Fisk plotted to bid up the price of gold (in greenbacks) in order to corner the market. They aimed to reap huge profits when they sold gold at advanced prices to merchants and others who needed it for foreign exchanges and customs duties. The chief governmental mechanism for preventing too high a rise in gold was sale of the metal on the New York exchange by the Treasury Department. For their scheme to work, therefore, Gould and Fisk had to be certain that the Treasury would stay out of the market. Working through Grant's brother-in-law, the two financiers met with the president and made the case that high-priced gold (or weak greenbacks) would help the nation's farmers increase their sales to foreign customers. Grant remained resolutely noncommittal in the spring and summer, but as the fall harvest approached, he became more impressed with the notion that a fall in gold prices would retard crop sales and hurt western farmers. Yet avoiding a fall in gold prices during the money crunch of harvest season was not the same as backing a rise. The conspirators proceeded with their work, but Grant soon urged his brother-in-law to cease speculating, and he warned Boutwell of "a desperate struggle" between "the bulls and bears" in New York. When the price of gold spiked at crisis levels in late September, the Treasury moved swiftly to sell gold, whose price quickly reverted to pre-conspiracy levels.[10]

A congressional investigation exonerated Grant of wrongdoing in the affair, although a Democratic minority report contained veiled hints of complicity by the president. Grant himself sought higher ground, using his first annual message to decry the swings in the greenback price of gold that made "the man of business an involuntary gambler." He called for legislation to "insure a gradual return to specie payments and put an immediate stop to fluctuations in the value of currency."[11] Still, Grant's critics assailed him for having anything at all to do with Gould and Fisk and portrayed the episode as one more example of his faulty judgment.

Nor were hard-money forces pleased by Grant's handling of legal challenges to the legitimacy of the greenbacks. In February 1870 the Supreme Court declared in *Hepburn v. Griswold* that the provision of the Legal Tender Act of 1862 that made the greenbacks valid for payment of debts incurred before the act was passed amounted to an unconstitutional impairment of contracts. Although hard-money advocates hailed the decision, Grant and Boutwell disagreed. By invalidating the use of greenbacks for a certain class of debts, the decision threatened to diminish their desirability, thereby undermining the administration's policy of gradually enhancing their value toward par. Virtually simultaneously with the release of the decision, Grant sent the Senate two nominations to fill vacancies on the Supreme Court with men known to disagree with the reasoning of the Court's slender majority. Shortly after the Senate confirmed the new justices, the administration initiated two new cases, and the reconstituted Court eventually reversed the *Hepburn* decision. Hard-money advocates were outraged, even though the later Court action checked the *Hepburn* decision's potential to destabilize the nation's currency. Overlooking Grant's long-term goal of achieving a safe return to specie payments, his critics (erroneously) accused him of "packing" the court in order to prop up a dangerous and illegitimate currency.

If the administration's monetary policy drew fire, so also did its fiscal policy. During the Civil War the federal government had enacted a wide array of new internal taxes and had substantially raised tariff rates. In the immediate postwar years, Congress eliminated or decreased a great many internal levies, but a movement for a similar reduction in the tariff failed. The customs levies not only generated revenue; they also gave American producers protection from foreign competition, protection that those producers desired to retain. Thus the wartime legislation had not only helped to entrench the protective principle in the nation's revenue structure; it had also placed the tariff at the center of fiscal debates for the remainder of the century.

The Democratic Party, dominated by its low-tariff southern wing, favored deep cuts in rates to levels necessary merely to meet the government's revenue requirements. Tariff reduction also appealed to some western Republicans in Congress whose agricultural constituents resented paying what they considered excessive tribute to eastern manufacturers. Also from within Grant's party, a group of "liberal" Republicans, some with ties to mercantile interests, wrapped their advocacy of lower customs duties in the mantle of "tariff reform." The president supported a decrease in the tariff and other taxes, but he gave higher priority to a steady repayment of the national debt. In his first annual message, in late 1869, he told Congress that internal levies and import duties should be reduced, but only after a refunding of the debt at a lower interest rate. With Grant's blessing, the Republican Congress passed compromise legislation that lowered some rates on raw materials and foodstuffs but left the duties on manufactures largely unchanged. After months of debate, this outcome convinced angry tariff "reformers" that the president had given in to the selfish demands of the nation's greedy protected interests.

On the other side of the fiscal ledger, the administration's spending policies also came under severe criticism. In January 1870 Massachusetts Republican Henry Dawes, chairman of the House Appropriations Committee, delivered a blistering attack on the proposals contained in Grant's first budget. Dawes had earlier told the president of his qualms about the increased spending estimates. Grant responded that at least for the War Department, whose needs he knew best, the estimates had been cut down as much as possible, and he suggested that Dawes meet with the secretaries of the other departments to see what economies could be reached. Instead, Dawes took to the House floor and complained that every department except the Post Office had requested an increase in spending over that in the last year of Johnson's term. Despite the administration's "professions of economy and reduction," Dawes charged, the proposed expenditures were "unjustifiable and without proper regard to economy or to the necessities of the case." For public works alone, the projected appropriations were four times greater. Grant's allies were stunned. In the House, Dawes's Massachusetts colleague, Benjamin F. Butler, asserted that in several instances Dawes's figures were misleading or erroneous. Johnson's estimates had been lower, Butler insisted, because of lingering surpluses from previous years and also because his department heads had purposely understated their projections to embarrass the incoming administration. Moreover, Butler charged that Dawes was too conservative and had only a meager understanding of the appropriations that "the necessities of a great nation and a great people require to be expended."[12] Grant himself was outraged by Dawes's sanctimonious lecture and thought his views befitted a Democrat more than a Republican. Nonetheless, the Appropriations chairman won plaudits as a champion of retrenchment, which had become the watchword in Congress and the nation at large.

Grant soon discovered that his foreign policy was no more exempt from criticism than his domestic policy. Early in his term he came in for a severe lashing for his attempt to annex the Dominican Republic, or Santo Domingo. This controversial initiative originated from within the Dominican government, which saw annexation as a way out of its chronic factionalism and oppressive debt. Although adventurers of shady character pushed the project, Grant dispatched his private secretary, Orville Babcock, to the island nation to investigate. Babcock returned with a draft annexation treaty, which, in modified form, the administration submitted to the Senate in early 1870. Grant saw great advantages to be gained from acquiring Santo Domingo: increased trade, a naval base ideally suited to defend a projected canal through Central America, a barrier to European ambitions in keeping with the Monroe Doctrine, and a potential refuge that would provide African Americans the opportunity to begin a new life or give them leverage to secure better treatment at home.

Once again Grant crossed swords with Charles Sumner, who as chairman of the Senate Foreign Relations Committee would exert powerful influence over the treaty's fate. The president took the unusual step of paying a private call on Sumner in his home to solicit his help. The senator's vague but courteous response led Grant to believe that Sumner would support annexation, but he was mistaken. Sumner led the majority of his committee in sending an adverse report on the treaty to the Senate floor, where the chairman delivered a ferocious diatribe against annexation. Sumner insisted that Santo Domingo was worthless to the United States, that taking over the government's debts would entail bottomless expense, and that annexation would lead to other island acquisitions equally useless and burdensome.

Undaunted, Grant lobbied mightily for the project, employing patronage and personal entreaty to win Senate converts. Sumner's friends relished the president's discomfiture. An American diplomat in London reported that "Henry Adams is over here telling everybody how weak the administration is and that Sumner is the only power in America."[13] In late June 1870 the Senate defeated the treaty by a vote of 28 to 28, falling far short of the necessary two-thirds. Nineteen Republicans abandoned the president. Grant later persuaded Congress to authorize a blue-ribbon commission, which duly reported on Santo Domingo's desirability, but the annexation project could not be revived. In the end, Grant's seemingly unjustified tenacity, coupled with rumors that some of his subordinates stood to gain financially from annexation, further eroded his support among the members of an emerging "reform" wing within the Republican Party.

The day after the treaty vote, Grant fired J. Lothrop Motley, a close ally of Sumner, from his post as minister to England. For some time Grant had contemplated removing Motley for insubordination, but the timing of the dismissal made it appear to be simply an act of pique, and it served only to deepen Sumner's animosity for the administration. Grant's frustration with Motley grew out of the minister's reluctance to follow State Department direction on another diplomatic front, the delicate negotiations with Great Britain for compensation for wartime depredations committed by Confederate vessels built in British shipyards. Throughout his tenure in London, Motley was less inclined to take his orders from the State Department than from Sumner. Early in Grant's term, Sumner jolted the Senate and the nation by demanding that Britain pay the United States not only for direct damages of some $15 million but an additional $2 billion to cover losses caused by the prolongation of the war occasioned by the operations of the *Alabama* and other British-built Confederate commerce raiders. This preposterous notion, parroted by Motley, angered the British and delayed serious negotiations for months. Unwilling to trust the erratic minister, Secretary of State Hamilton Fish transferred the negotiations to the United States, where in May 1871 they resulted in the Treaty of Washington, by which the two nations submitted the outstanding issues to arbitration. This outcome was a signal triumph for the administration and for the principle of the peaceful settlement of international disputes, but Grant's critics were loath to give him much credit for the success.

While these domestic and foreign policy issues occupied much of the attention of the government in Washington, sectional and racial resentment continued to infect the South. The violence that had marred the election of 1868 continued into 1869 and 1870, and southern Republicans looked to leaders in Washington for help. The Fifteenth Amendment achieved ratification by the end of March 1870, but the amendment was not self-executing, and in May, Congress passed an Enforcement Act to throw federal protection around the right to vote. Echoing the amendment, the law outlawed discrimination in voting based on race, color, or previous condition of servitude, and it prohibited interference with voting by force, intimidation, bribery, or economic sanction. It also included provisions to undergird the protections outlined in the Fourteenth Amendment. The law passed by a strict party vote, with northern Democrats signaling their solid allegiance to southern white conservatives who were resisting social and political change. Yet even though Republicans in Congress voted as a unit for the bill, some, such as Senator Carl Schurz of Missouri, warned against "undue centralization" and argued that giving the president the "power to surround the polls with the military forces of the United States" was "repugnant to the genius of free institutions." Thus, despite Grant's hope that ratification of the Fifteenth Amendment would take matters of black suffrage and reconstruction "out of politics," these issues remained at the center of political contention.[14]

Like most presidents in the late nineteenth century, Grant soon found that the patronage power was as much a burden as a boon for any chief executive who tried to use the bestowal of office to unite his party or promote his policy agenda. After his initial experiment with independence in making appointments, Grant began to pay closer attention to the recommendations from members of Congress who embraced his policies. Inevitably, the choices he made bound some men closer to the administration and alienated others. In some states, appointments served to exacerbate rather than allay party divisions, and civil service reformers claimed to see a disturbing tendency to select officeholders on the basis of factional loyalty rather than fitness and merit. In June 1870 Grant dismayed reformers when he replaced his attorney general, the Massachusetts Brahmin E. R. Hoar, with a southerner as part of his larger effort to curry favor in certain quarters for his Santo Domingo project.

The civil service question took an ugly turn in the fall of 1870 with the resignation of Secretary of the Interior Jacob D. Cox. Cox had won praise from reformers for instituting appointment examinations in some Interior Department offices and also for protecting departmental employees from assessments against their salaries by Republican Party fund-raisers. As the fall congressional elections approached, Cox refused to permit clerks to take leave to return to their home districts to assist in the campaign and vote, although such leaves were common practice in the government. When Grant reversed Cox's order, the secretary submitted his resignation. The two men had previously clashed on an unrelated claims matter, and now Grant decided to accept the departure of Cox. In retaliation, Cox published their private correspondence on the civil service issue. Reformers applauded Cox while Grant's supporters branded him as a traitor. "The correspondence between Mr. Cox and the President," lamented veteran Republican senator Henry Wilson, "is damaging to us beyond measure."[15]

Wilson may have exaggerated, but the Republicans did see their fortunes decline in the 1870 elections. They lost state elections in the key swing states of Indiana and New York. In Missouri, critics of Grant, led by Senator Carl Schurz and calling themselves liberal Republicans, allied with Democrats and elected Benjamin Gratz Brown as governor. In elections for the national House of Representatives, the Republicans suffered a net loss of thirty-five seats, reducing their proportion of seats from 70 to 56 percent. Such a decline was not unusual for a midterm election, but reformers were quick to attribute it to popular discontent with Grant's supposed opposition to reform.

That assertion was overdrawn, but the president moved swiftly to head off further revolt within the GOP on the civil service issue. Although he thought his critics' discontent derived mostly from their disappointment at their own failure to receive patronage recognition, Grant used his December 1870 annual message to project himself forward as a champion of reform. Declaring that the current system of congressional patronage did "not secure the best men, and often not even fit men, for public service," he called for the "elevation and purification of the civil service of the Government."[16] Congress responded by authorizing the president to appoint a commission to devise a merit system, and Grant chose the renowned reformer George William Curtis as its chairman. Once the group had written a body of rules governing competitive examinations and other improvements, Grant promptly put them into operation. Within Congress, however, support remained lukewarm among those Republicans who, though they might deplore the onerous burden of dispensing offices, hesitated to relinquish the influence and political advantage that the practice gave them.

Although reformers claimed primacy for the civil service issue in the 1870 elections, several forces were at play, including the Democrats' recapture of more than fifteen congressional seats in the reconstructed South. Despite the passage of the Enforcement Act in May, violence or the threat of violence had a telling impact in several states, especially Georgia, Alabama, and North Carolina. In his annual message Grant asserted that intimidation or overt violence had undermined the right of suffrage in some areas and had thus subverted the voters' will. The mayhem did not diminish in the ensuing months. The situation had grown so grave by the time the new Congress assembled in March 1871 that Grant took the unusual step of convening a meeting of cabinet members and congressional leaders at the Capitol, where he asked for further authority to meet the crisis.

In the ensuing prolonged congressional debate over proposed legislation, Democrats maintained that the violence had been exaggerated, if not wholly imagined, but they also made the contradictory argument that bad government by the Reconstruction regimes had sparked the disorders. Most Republicans saw the threat as real, citing specific outrages perpetrated by the Ku Klux Klan and similar organizations. Whereas the Democrats warned against an unwarranted expansion of federal power, Republicans were willing to go to the extreme limits of constitutional authority to ensure the protection of life and liberty as guaranteed by the new amendments to the Constitution. A minority of Republicans, however, sided with the Democrats, especially in opposing a provision to empower the president to suspend the writ of habeas corpus and institute martial law in violence-plagued regions. Carl Schurz, who had emerged as a national leader of Grant's liberal Republican critics, argued that enlarging the executive's power to deal with the disorders threatened to "pervert our system of government" and "expose the constitutional rights of the people to the vicissitudes of partisan tyranny."[17] Nonetheless, Grant's allies prevailed. The Ku Klux Klan Act, passed in April 1871, outlawed conspiracy to deprive persons of their constitutional rights and stated that in cases of violence or conspiracy where states either failed or refused to protect individuals' rights, the president could employ the army to do so and if necessary suspend the writ of habeas corpus.

Under this legislation, federal officials launched a prosecutorial effort in several parts of the South. In October 1871 Grant suspended the writ in nine South Carolina counties, and federal troops made hundreds of arrests. These actions against the Klan demoralized the organization, and incidents of violence declined, at least temporarily. Back in Washington, Grant and Congress offered an olive branch in the form of legislation, passed in the spring of 1872, conferring amnesty on virtually all ex-Confederates. But Democrats and Republican defectors blocked an effort by Charles Sumner to put additional civil rights legislation on the books.

As the presidential election of 1872 approached, liberal Republicans remained unreconciled to Grant, despite his launching of civil service reform and acceptance of Confederate amnesty, two key items on the reformers' agenda. Recognizing that they could not hope to block Grant's renomination, they held their own nominating convention under the banner of a new Liberal Republican Party. But true reformers formed only one contingent at the oddly mixed gathering. Among the delegates were free traders and protectionists, civil service reformers and disappointed spoilsmen, and other diverse elements, whose single common bond was a desire to oust Grant. After a jumbled fight for the presidential nomination, in which front-runner Charles Francis Adams, former minister to England and father of Henry, refused to dicker for delegates, the convention turned to Horace Greeley, editor of the *New York Tribune*. The

choice bordered on the bizarre. Greeley could not boast any real
civil service reform credentials, and on the tariff he had long championed protectionism. Many genuine reformers balked at supporting
his candidacy. After the convention, E. L. Godkin wrote to Carl
Schurz that Greeley was "a conceited, ignorant, half cracked, obstinate
old creature" whose election to the presidency would be "a national
calamity."[18]

The convention's platform failed to mollify many who were disenchanted by the nomination. The resolutions committee, under
pressure from Greeley, dodged the tariff issue by simply saying that
Congress should decide it. Within a few weeks Congress passed
legislation eliminating or lowering duties on raw materials and reducing those on manufactured goods by 10 percent, thereby depriving the Liberals of any real political benefit from the issue. The
Liberal Republican platform endorsed civil service reform in general terms but ignored Grant's genuine efforts and offered nothing
specific beyond limiting the president to a single term. As for Grant's
Reconstruction policy, the Liberals called for the reining in of "military authority" and "a return to the methods of peace."[19]

On the eve of the regular Republican convention, Charles Sumner took to the Senate floor to deliver a stinging, if contradictory,
indictment of the president. On the one hand, the senator accused
Grant of laziness, incompetence, and treating the presidential office
"as little more than a plaything . . . where palace cars, fast horses,
and sea-side loiterings figure more than duties." On the other hand,
Sumner denounced the president for being too strong, showing an
overweening "Caesarism," by which "the safeguards of constitutional government were subordinated to the personal pretensions of
One Man."[20] If anything, such rantings attached the Republican
delegates even more steadfastly to their chief, who won a unanimous
renomination on a platform that applauded his leadership and endorsed his policies.

Desperate to dethrone Grant, the Democrats nominated Greeley
and adopted the Liberal platform verbatim. The country thus witnessed

the spectacle of Greeley, a longtime unrelenting critic of the Democrats, now carrying their banner. With issues such as the tariff and civil service effectively neutralized, Greeley focused on sectional reconciliation. He broke precedent and took a campaign speaking tour, during which he denounced Republican Reconstruction policies and urged Americans to "clasp hands across the bloody chasm." Grant did not campaign, but his Republican surrogates portrayed Greeley as a dupe of his new Democratic allies. Republicans accepted amnesty for ex-Confederates and praised the return of fraternal feelings, but they also cited abundant evidence of white southerners' continued recalcitrance. As long as "they *allow* scourgings and torture, and murder of innocent men," one Republican speaker insisted, "they cannot expect peace."[21]

Although some Democrats claimed to embrace a "new departure" in sectional and race relations, the former abolitionist Greeley employed campaign rhetoric tinged with racism. Noting that the recent constitutional amendments had settled the issue of rights for the former slaves, he argued that the question had now become whether "the white man of this country shall have equal rights with the black men." His running mate, Benjamin Gratz Brown, warned of turning the government over to "a negro population, largely ignorant of the laws of wealth, of society, [and] of civil government." Even Sumner, the nation's foremost defender of the rights of blacks, allowed his hatred of Grant to drive him to call for sectional "reconciliation . . . instead of *irritating antagonism*" and to declare that "the surest trust of the colored people is in Horace Greeley." Unmoved, Frederick Douglass urged his fellow African Americans to reject Sumner's "insidious and dangerous advice" and stand by Grant.[22]

Grant defeated Greeley by 55.6 percent to 43.8 percent of the popular vote, and the president garnered 286 electoral votes out of a total of 366. In the congressional elections, the Republicans maintained a two-thirds control of each house.

Substantial as this victory was, however, Republicans failed to achieve a lasting realignment in the electorate. Even before the election, the era's first major scandal, the Crédit Mobilier, cast a taint upon the party. The directors of the Union Pacific Railroad had created the Crédit Mobilier to carry out the line's construction, which, underwritten by government bonds, promised to yield huge profits for them. To deter congressional snooping, railroad promoter and Massachusetts Republican congressman Oakes Ames allegedly distributed company stock at bargain prices to key party leaders, including Grant's vice president, Schuyler Colfax, as well as Henry Dawes and James A. Garfield. Although a House investigation went no further than to censure Ames and one colleague, the incident besmirched the GOP's image. So also did a bill passed in the waning hours of the Forty-second Congress to raise federal salaries, a raise that in the case of congressmen and senators would be retroactive for two years. This so-called Salary Grab evoked an outcry, and although the next Congress rescinded it, the political damage was done. The Democrats, however, were hardly pristine. Many of them had also voted for the raise, and their party still bore the disgrace of the recently exposed Tammany Hall ring headed by Boss William M. Tweed in New York.

More damaging than scandal for the Republicans was the economic crisis triggered in September 1873 by the downfall of the banking firm of Jay Cooke and Company. Years of good times in the country had fueled overheated speculation, which wise heads knew could not last forever. The bubble burst when the esteemed banking house, overextended in unprofitable investments, could not meet its obligations and closed its doors. Other banks soon followed Cooke into collapse, and the Panic of 1873 sparked a depression that lasted for five years. In the absence of a central bank or the Federal Reserve (still four decades in the future), the government lacked the agility to allay the crisis. The Treasury released $26 million from its greenback reserve, but this afforded only minor and temporary relief. Grant called upon Congress to devise methods to achieve

Panic grips Wall Street in New York the day after Jay Cooke and Company closed its doors. (Library of Congress)

greater elasticity in the currency, but he warned against "undue inflation." Nonetheless, after a contentious debate in the spring of 1874, Congress passed a bill to increase greenback circulation by $44 million and national banknotes by $46 million. The measure pitted hard- and soft-money supporters against each other in both parties, and the debate betrayed sectional divisions between the East against the bill and the West and South for it. Tempted at first to sign it in order to mollify western and southern opinion, Grant finally vetoed the Inflation Bill. Warning against the evils of an irredeemable currency, he decried the bill's call for an additional $100 million in paper circulation as "a departure from true principles of finance, national interest, [and] national obligations to creditors." The veto was one of the few acts by Grant that hard-money liberal reformers applauded, but many inflationist Republicans believed, as one reporter put it, that the president had "stabbed the party to death."[23]

Hard times haunted the Republicans' prospects for the congressional elections later in the year. So, too, did continued troubles in the South. Worried over their own fading economic prospects, many northerners felt diminished solicitude for the former slaves, whose abuse and exploitation by white southern conservatives federal authorities seemed unable to stop. Six weeks after Grant's second inauguration, Colfax, Louisiana, witnessed the worst racial violence in all Reconstruction, savagery that left more than a hundred African Americans dead.

In general, the tangled politics of Louisiana epitomized the difficulty of managing Reconstruction from Washington. In the disputed outcome of the state elections of 1872, the dominant Grant Republicans claimed victory, but so did the Democrats, who had joined with a breakaway Republican faction. Grant accepted a court order upholding the Republican state administration, but the Democrats remained unreconciled. They began forming so-called White Leagues to root out Republican rule, thereby launching a movement that spread to other southern states. In September 1874 the White Leaguers staged a bloody coup in New Orleans and seized control of the state government. Although Grant had previously been drifting away from an aggressive interventionist policy, he refused to recognize the new regime and threatened to use armed force against it. The insurgents soon backed down, but the underlying problem of white conservative defiance persisted.

Meanwhile, more allegations of corruption surfaced, including the so-called Sanborn contracts. In the spring of 1874 an investigation revealed that lax collection of taxes by regular Treasury officials had opened the way for John Sanborn, operating as a special tax collector under contract, to amass more than $200,000 in commissions, some of which apparently went into the campaign coffers of his political patron, a Republican congressman. Threatened by congressional censure, Treasury secretary William A. Richardson, who had replaced Boutwell, resigned. Although Grant replaced Richardson with the impeccably honest Benjamin Bristow and Congress moved to end the commission system, the episode further eroded the GOP's prospects.

As the 1874 congressional elections approached, Republicans could not escape from the general disenchantment of a public turned off by hard times, scandal, and continued disorder in the South. The Democrats hammered away at these issues and won a substantial majority in the House of Representatives, giving them control of the chamber for the first time since before the Civil War. Although the Democrats gained seats in every region of the country, the result especially confirmed their dominance in the South, where they won nearly half their seats and boasted eighty-nine representatives to seventeen for the Republicans.

In the last session of the previous, Forty-third Congress, from December 1874 to early March 1875, the Republicans strove to enact as much of their agenda as possible before relinquishing power. In an effort to defuse the volatile currency issue and to unify the party's hard- and soft-money wings, they passed the Specie Resumption Act in early January. The measure set January 1, 1879, as the date the Treasury would begin redeeming greenbacks in gold. It removed the limits on the issuance of national banknotes but stipulated that for every $100 in new notes, the Treasury would withdraw $80 in greenbacks, until the total volume of greenbacks was reduced to $300 million. The bill's sponsor, John Sherman, claimed that it would effect resumption with neither inflation nor deflation and bring a new stability to the nation's money supply. Democrats opposed the measure as doing little to revive the economy, but the Republicans pushed it through both houses by a party-line vote. After years of wrangling, Congress had at last set a date certain for specie resumption.

The other major piece of legislation that passed during the short session was the Civil Rights Act of 1875. Charles Sumner, who had pushed for such legislation for years, had died the previous spring, and the Senate passed his bill in part as a memorial to the fallen champion of black rights. But the bill's provision for equality in public schools could not clear the House, and as finally passed in February, it outlawed discrimination in inns, public conveyances, theaters and other places of amusement, and jury selection. Inadequate enforcement mechanisms rendered the measure fatally weak, and the Supreme Court declared it unconstitutional in 1883. As the congressional session drew to a close, the House approved a bill to strengthen the president's hand in defending voting rights in the South, but the Senate refused to go along. The dilution of the civil rights bill and the failure of new enforcement legislation reflected the growing sense of futility among Republicans at the prospects of achieving lasting change in the South.

That feeling was exacerbated in early January, when, in the midst of a fracas over contested seats in the Louisiana legislature, federal troops marched in and removed several Democratic members not duly elected. This supposed violation of republican principles by a military contingent sparked a national uproar, and protest meetings across the North featured prominent Republican speakers as well as Democrats. Although Grant defended the soldiers' actions as warranted by the provocation, he could read the popular mood as well as anyone. Coupled with the Republicans' loss of the House, the incident in New Orleans killed the prospects for any new Reconstruction initiative.

When the last session of the Forty-third Congress was gaveled to a close on March 3, 1875, Republican hegemony in the federal government came to an end. The Grant administration, which had begun with high hopes for the party and the nation, had navigated a sea of troubles. Reconstruction was unraveling and widely discredited, and the economy lay in tatters, largely for reasons beyond the politicians' power to control. Grant spent his last two years in office with the House dominated by the Democrats, who lost few opportunities to undermine his administration. The nation had entered a period of divided government that would last for more than a decade. In addition, the two major parties moved toward equilibrium in national strength, with the Democrats tightening their grip on the South and the Republicans solidifying power through much of the North and West.

TWO

Hayes: Uncertain Triumph

After the adjournment of Congress in early March 1875, politicians of both parties watched the spring elections in several states to gauge their standing with the public. In municipal elections in Indiana, Republicans did well, but in New Hampshire the GOP candidate for governor squeaked by his Democratic opponent by fewer than two hundred votes. The Republicans fared even worse in Connecticut, where congressional elections turned the state's House delegation from three-to-one Republican to three-to-one Democratic. Postmaster General Marshall Jewell, himself a Connecticut Republican, attributed the party's continued ill fortunes to a variety of causes, but he pointed especially to hard times. "Everything is at a stand still," he wrote the American minister in Paris. Yet Jewell was also alarmed by "a growing feeling of distrust of our Administration. We have been pelted away by the newspapers, and so much has been said about the Administration that it does have some effect." "I wish," he added, "some of our friends could see the importance of the cleaning out process, but I am afraid they cannot."[1]

Jewell's fears proved justified, for allegations of official wrongdoing continued to surface. In the summer of 1875 Interior secretary Columbus Delano resigned amid charges that his son had received unlawful payments in the form of compensation for work he failed to perform or bribes from individuals seeking favorable treatment by the Interior Department. That year also witnessed a full-scale assault on the so-called Whiskey Ring by Secretary of the Treasury Benjamin Bristow. Dating back many years, the ring was a widespread conspiracy of distillers and government agents who had defrauded the government of millions of dollars in excise taxes and had operated with the connivance of revenue officials in Washington. Bristow raided many of the nation's largest distilleries and pursued a yearlong legal battle that netted scores of convictions. The secretary won public gratitude for his crusade, but even though the ring originated before Grant took office, its existence added one more black mark against his administration of the government.

Nor did Grant's handling of the civil service question burnish his image, especially with reformers. Although Grant privately questioned some aspects of the rules devised by the Civil Service Commission, he considered the reform valuable and repeatedly asked Congress for legislation to "render the enforcement of the system binding upon my successors." Republican legislators showed little disposition to take that step, however. Finally, exasperated both by Congress's meager appropriations and by reformers' persistent faultfinding, Grant declared in December 1874 that if Congress adjourned without "positive legislation" on civil service, he would abandon the commission. The legislature took no action, and the president abolished the rules in March 1875. The depth of Grant's sincerity in backing the reform became a subject of debate, but neither its champions nor its opponents found much to applaud.[2]

By the spring of 1875, many Republicans could scarcely disguise their anxiety that the president would seek another term. Even Vice President Henry Wilson concluded that Grant was "more unpopular than Andrew Johnson was in his darkest days" and saw him as a "mill-stone around the neck of our party that would sink it out of sight." Initially the president thought it unseemly to take notice of the question, but when state party leaders pushed for some definitive statement, Grant declared in late May that he would not be a candidate for renomination. Many Republicans breathed a sigh of relief, but the declination distressed some, including the great African American leader Frederick Douglass, who regarded Grant as "the shelter and savior of my people in the hour of supreme danger."[3]

Douglass's was a minority view on the southern question, however, for overall the GOP moved farther away from the interventionist policy. This pulling back became manifest in the administration's handling of the threatened disruption of the state election in Mississippi in the fall of 1875. Fearing violence by white paramilitary units, the Republican governor, Adelbert Ames, requested Grant to intervene. Away from Washington, the president relied on Attorney General Edwards Pierrepont to coordinate the administration's response. Pierrepont, a New Yorker with a moderate reform record, was wary of offending anti-interventionist opinion in the North and misled Grant about the severity of the situation in Mississippi. The president ordered the preparation of a presidential proclamation justifying intervention in case of need, but at Pierrepont's urging, it was not issued. Ames was left to his own devices. Pierrepont dispatched an agent who worked out a peace agreement of sorts between Ames and his enemies, but at election time, the white conservatives nonetheless carried out a reign of terror, and the Democrats emerged victorious.

Pierrepont and many other GOP strategists were looking beyond 1875 toward the presidential election of 1876. In their view, Mississippi, with its eight electoral votes, along with other southern states now in the grasp of the Democrats, seemed far less critical than a northern powerhouse such as Ohio, whose twenty-two votes would be indispensable to GOP victory. In Ohio's state elections in 1875, the southern question faded and other issues came to the fore. Although state governments had no direct role in currency matters, that issue became a central feature of the Ohio campaign, during which

soft-money Democrats played into the hands of Republicans who
sought to identify their own party with monetary orthodoxy. For
governor the Democrats renominated the seventy-one-year-old incumbent, William Allen, who had entered politics as a hard-money
Jacksonian but now fervently embraced the greenbacks and opposed
currency contraction. The Democratic state convention demanded
that the policy of the Specie Resumption Act be abandoned, that the
national banks be abolished and replaced by state banks, and that
paper currency be exclusively issued by the government.

Conservative Republicans could hardly have asked for a better
foil. To oppose Allen, the GOP tapped former governor and congressman Rutherford B. Hayes, a former Union general who had been
wounded five times during the Civil War. Hayes was a popular politician and a proven vote getter who had first won the governorship in
1867 despite a general Democratic tide that year. An effective speaker
on the stump, he attacked the Democrats' monetary notions as economic and moral iniquity. "Every period of inflation," Hayes declared, "is followed by a loss of confidence, a shrinkage of values,
depression of business, panics, lack of employment, and widespread
disaster and distress." Hayes recognized that "there are localities
where our position on [the] currency question will be damaging, but
on the whole it must help. At any rate, we are right." As for southern
affairs, he had concluded that "'the let-alone policy' seems now to
be the true course." The Republican Party's leading orators, including the erstwhile Liberal Carl Schurz, flocked to Ohio to help Hayes
wage the battle for a sound currency.[4]

Hayes and the Ohio Republicans supplemented their economic
attacks by charging the Democrats with improper subservience to the
Catholic Church. In the spring the Democratic state legislature had
passed a law that stipulated that inmates in state prisons and patients
in state hospitals were entitled to receive religious instruction in
their own faiths and that the institutions should provide equal facili-
ties for such instruction. Although the act was designed to sanction

the assignment of Catholic chaplains, Republicans played on Protestant worries and cast it as the entering wedge to divert part of the state's educational funds to parochial schools. Over the years, some American Catholics had advocated such a policy, but Ohio's Democratic platform sought to distance the party from that position by flatly opposing the "division among or control by any sect, directly or indirectly, of any portion of the Public School Fund." Still, Republicans continued to press the issue, and two weeks before the Ohio election President Grant urged Americans to "encourage free schools, and resolve that not one dollar of money appropriated to their support, no matter how raised, shall be appropriated to the support of any sectarian school."[5]

In the October gubernatorial election, Hayes won a narrow victory over Allen, and the Republicans carried a majority in both houses of the state legislature. Hayes's success thrust him forward as a potential presidential candidate and also fired the enthusiasm of Republicans in other state contests in November. In Pennsylvania, where the currency issue largely replicated the debate in Ohio, the Republicans won a substantial victory. The party also did well in other northern states, including the key swing state of New York. Overall, the outcome in 1875 represented an impressive comeback after the party's heavy losses the previous year. Republican optimists such as Pierrepont concluded that the results "*insure a* Republican success in 1876 so far as human foresight can look." Although the southern question had not dropped completely from sight in the campaign, especially in states where the parties showed scant difference on the currency question, the elections of 1875 suggested a declining importance for sectional issues. When Congress convened in December, Grant and other Republicans sought to keep the schools issue alive by proposing constitutional amendments to bar the sectarian use of public educational funds. Treasury secretary Bristow thought that the elections' most important lesson was that "the question of finance is to be the controlling one in politics."

Similarly, Ohio congressman James A. Garfield believed that the outcome had weakened but not expunged inflationist doctrines, and that "we shall see another hard struggle over that issue, and it will be a wider, and more hotly contested fight than any we have yet had."[6]

As the presidential election year of 1876 unfolded, however, neither of these new issues played quite the role predicted. In the House of Representatives the Democratic majority sent the school-funding amendment to committee, where it remained bottled up for most of the session. The currency issue occupied a considerable portion of Congress's time, but sectional differences on the question exposed the dangers either party would encounter in focusing on it in a national election campaign. Soft-money House Democrats, largely from the West, pushed repeatedly for repeal of the Specie Resumption Act, but each time, they were defeated by a combination of hard-money eastern Democrats and the preponderance of Republicans. Moreover, the spring witnessed the first significant discussion of the silver question. In the winter of 1873, in a move little noticed at the time, Congress had dropped the silver dollar from the list of the nation's coins. The coin had fallen into disuse, but the discovery and extraction of large silver stocks in the Far West kindled a new movement on its behalf. Silver mining interests as well as inflationists eager to spur the economy began to condemn the Coinage Act of 1873 as the "Crime of '73" and to push for the "remonetization" of silver. Their favored measure called for the coinage of silver dollars at a ratio of sixteen to one with gold dollars. But because gold was worth more on the open market than this proposed official coinage ratio indicated, hard-money men warned that such a program would drain the Treasury of gold. The silver coinage proposal got nowhere in Congress.

As matters turned out, neither school funding nor the currency dominated the 1876 campaign. Instead, questions related to the South and to reform took center stage. The assembling of the Forty-fourth Congress in December 1875 gave Republicans stark notice of what they had lost in the 1874 elections. Sixty-one former Confederate officers sat across the aisle in the new Democratic House, and the chairmen of twenty-one of the thirty-four most important committees came from the former slave states. "This," Garfield noted with scorn, "is the old Southern Rule returning again with a vengeance."[7] The new situation heightened Republicans' anxiety over the coming election and underscored the dire necessity of preserving their hold on the presidency. A Democrat in the White House, Republicans believed, would do nothing to restrain southern whites' violation of blacks' rights, especially the right to vote. And should the Democrats gain control of both houses of Congress as well as the presidency, they would repeal civil rights legislation wholesale.

Early in the congressional session, Democrats presented a bill for amnesty for all ex-Confederates disqualified from holding office by the Fourteenth Amendment. Such a bill had passed the previous Republican House, but now former speaker James G. Blaine offered an amendment to exclude Jefferson Davis, not because Davis had headed the rebellion, but because he was ultimately accountable for the horrible abuses at the Confederate prison at Andersonville. A representative from Maine since 1863, Blaine had risen rapidly in the ranks and, as speaker from 1869 to 1875, had earned bipartisan respect for his evenhanded management of the House. Moreover, he was a popular spokesman for the Republican Party throughout the country, and he exhibited a winning personal charm. "Had he been a woman," one contemporary noted, "people would have rushed off to send expensive flowers."[8] Yet he had also made a good many enemies over the years, and he could be daunting in debate.

In the amnesty discussion, Blaine's aim was not to prevent Jefferson Davis from returning to office, never even a remote possibility, but to test the "real feelings" of the southerners in the House. Many of them leaped to the bait, blaming the miseries at Andersonville on northern actions and generally defending Davis and the Confederacy. Although the bitter debate had an artificial character, the southerners' attitude and bearing confirmed Republicans' dread of Democratic rule. So too did a Democratic effort to attach to an appropriation bill a rider that would have repealed key provisions of voting rights enforcement laws passed earlier in the decade. "I think," wrote a seasoned GOP journalist, "the Republican party with all its rings and rascals is Heaven to the Hell of a restored Democracy."[9]

Yet fresh news of "rings and rascals" continued to undermine the Republicans' claim to moral high ground on the southern question. In February 1876, federal prosecutors in St. Louis put Grant's private secretary, Orville Babcock, on trial on charges of complicity in the Whiskey Ring. The evidence, which included coded telegrams, was damning. By this time Grant had borne unremitting criticism from reformers for years. One may speculate how much these travails had clouded his judgment regarding a close subordinate like Babcock, who had been by his side since the war. As Secretary of State Hamilton Fish observed, the president felt that "the prosecution was aimed at himself, & that they were putting him on trial."[10] As the trial approached, Grant seemed determined to testify on Babcock's behalf, and only the insistence of his cabinet led him to give a deposition instead. Largely on the weight of Grant's statement, the jury acquitted Babcock, but that outcome hardly diminished the new opprobrium that fell upon the president. Punctuating this bleak period for the president, just a week later Secretary of War William W. Belknap stunned Grant with his abrupt resignation in the face of certain impeachment for accepting bribes.

Many other men connected with the administration came under scrutiny by congressional Democrats who had taken control of the investigative machinery of the House committees. That naked partisanship motivated much of the Democrats' anticorruption zeal seemed obvious when they launched inquiries of clearly scrupulous officials, including Bristow, Fish, and Postmaster General Marshall Jewell. An American diplomat in Paris likened the "fury of 'investigation' in Washington" to "the days of the French Revolution when it was enough to cry 'suspect'—& the man was ruined."[11]

Whether individual charges were fair or not, the corruption issue presented Republicans with an image crisis of immense proportions. Inevitably, the orgy of crimination affected the contest for the party's presidential nomination. Candidates closely associated with the administration, such as New York's Roscoe Conkling and Indiana's Oliver P. Morton, hardly seemed suited to carry the banner of reform. In a crowded field, James G. Blaine emerged as the front-runner, but in April, press reports carried allegations that he had profited handsomely from dealings with railroads in exchange for favorable treatment while he served as House Speaker. A congressional investigation, led by southern Democrats who had been irritated by Blaine's speech about Jefferson Davis, uncovered embarrassing evidence, especially a series of letters held by one James Mulligan, the former bookkeeper of one of the railroad men with whom Blaine had dealt. In a bold move, Blaine secured possession of the letters from Mulligan. At a dramatic House session in early June, he held the packet of letters high above his head, declared, "Thank God Almighty I am not ashamed to show them," and proceeded to read them to his colleagues and the packed galleries.[12] Although the letters did not show that Blaine had breached the prevailing ethical standards in Congress, they revealed a man bent on improving his own financial interests. In a masterstroke, Blaine turned the tables on his Democratic inquisitors, charging them (accurately) with suppressing exculpatory evidence, and he convinced many people that he was the victim of unfair delving into his private affairs. Still, although Blaine's candidacy remained alive, it suffered from the blow, and despite his enormous abilities as a party leader, the taint of corruption hung about him for the rest of his life.

As the swirl of allegations threatened to engulf the GOP, many reform-minded members of the party moved to rescue it from disaster. Still smarting from the Greeley fiasco in 1872, these Republicans now believed it better to try to regenerate the party from within. They gravitated toward the ring-fighting Bristow as the ideal presidential candidate. In mid-May, while the Blaine drama was unfolding, leaders from business, academe, politics, and the professions had gathered in New York for a conference to consider the prospects for a reformation of public life. The group's official statement urged the selection of a new president who possessed "the moral courage and sturdy resolution to grapple with abuses which have acquired the strength of established custom."[13] The statement did not mention the Treasury secretary by name, although the reformers' preference was clear. But such an endorsement, even by implication, was the kiss of death in the eyes of the Grant people, many of whom—including the president himself—considered Bristow a traitor to the administration.

When the Republican National Convention met in mid-June, Blaine still held a substantial lead in delegates. In a memorable nominating speech, one of his supporters referred to the Maine statesman as a "plumed knight" doing battle against his personal detractors and the enemies of his country. The sobriquet stuck, but it proved insufficient to overcome suspicions about Blaine's character. Bristow's advocates, including former Civil Service Commission chairman George William Curtis, hailed the secretary's crusading honesty and likened the current "political corruption and demoralization" to the "mortal peril" of slavery two decades earlier. Ironically, the Bristow supporters' emphasis on the ethics issue played into the hands of the supporters of Rutherford B. Hayes. The issue was strong enough to raise fatal doubts about Blaine and about Grant's allies, Morton and Conkling, but it also aggravated the contempt those men's defenders felt for Bristow. Recognizing their opening, Hayes's backers portrayed the Ohio governor as a perfectly clean public servant "against whom nothing can be said" and who also had "no personal enemies." Ultimately, the reformers and the pro-administration forces combined their strength to defeat Blaine, who narrowly lost to Hayes on the seventh ballot.[14]

In their platform the Republicans hailed "the quickened conscience of the people concerning political affairs" and promised that the "punishment of all who betray official trusts shall be speedy, thorough, and unsparing." On the civil service question, the platform called for the selection of appointees on the basis of "honesty, fidelity, and capacity." Arraigning Democrats for "applauding in the national capitol the sentiments of unrepentant rebellion," the Republicans called for the "permanent pacification" of the South and the "complete protection of all its citizens" under the recent constitutional amendments. Reprising an issue from 1875, they endorsed an amendment banning the use of public funds for sectarian schools. In a gingerly treatment of the money question, the platform demanded "a continuous and steady progress to specie payment" but did not mention the Specie Resumption Act by name. More forthrightly, it recommended a tariff "so adjusted as to promote the interests of American labor and advance the prosperity of the whole country."[15]

In the preconvention maneuvering on the Democratic side, the odds-on favorite was Samuel J. Tilden, who had won the governorship of New York handily in the Democratic sweep of 1874. A wealthy railroad lawyer, Tilden was an accomplished wireworker in New York politics and had chaired the state party since 1866. His legendary organizational skills made him a hero to his party allies, but his outsmarted opponents vilified him as "Slippery Sam." When the Tweed Ring in New York City became an embarrassment to the Democrats, Tilden joined the movement for its overthrow, as much to salvage his party as to cleanse it. As governor, he further burnished his image as a reformer by breaking the so-called Canal Ring, a band of corruptionists defrauding the state's canal system. As a crusading alternative to the tainted Republicans and as a prominent figure in the nation's largest swing state, Tilden emerged by early 1876 as a formidable presidential candidate. His forces dominated the national convention in late June in St. Louis, where he easily secured the nomination on the second ballot. Tilden's principal opponent, Thomas A. Hendricks of Indiana, received the second spot on the ticket.

Hendricks's nomination for vice president highlighted the chief obstacle Tilden confronted—division in the Democratic Party over the currency question. Tilden favored hard money while Hendricks was a leading midwestern voice for inflation. This attempt at balance could easily result in one end of the ticket repelling the supporters of the other. The convention tried to paper over the differences in a platform that called for the repeal of the specie resumption clause of the 1875 law, not because the policy was wrong, but because the act itself stood as a hindrance to resumption. After the convention, Hendricks continued to call for resumption repeal as a positive good, moving Tilden to labor mightily to ensure that the two nominees' letters of acceptance at least roughly coincided on the issue in the same vein as the platform. Given the intraparty dissonance on the money question, Tilden was convinced that the Democrats' best strategy was to turn "the whole public attention" to "the reform issue on which we are united, and on which our antagonists can not resist us or defend themselves." The platform, drafted by a close Tilden ally, repeatedly invoked the phrase "reform is necessary" in introducing not only the plank calling for "a sound currency" but others dealing with such issues as the tariff, civil service, and the South.[16]

Following custom, the nominees did not take campaign speaking tours but instead offered their views in formal public letters accepting nomination. Eager to tap reform sentiment, Hayes opened with a lengthy discussion of the civil service, decrying the prevailing practice of partisan patronage and calling for a reform that was "thorough, radical, and complete." On the money question, in language suggested by Carl Schurz, he favored a speedy resumption of specie payments and argued that an end to uncertainty regarding currency values was essential to revive business confidence and restore prosperity. On the South, Hayes called for "peace" and endorsed a federal policy designed to secure "the blessings of honest and capable local government" in the formerly seceded states, thereby indicating that he would back away from military intervention. He emphasized, however, that such a shift would be contingent upon southerners' recognition of the rights embodied in the Thirteenth, Fourteenth, and Fifteenth amendments. "All parts of the Constitution are sacred and must be sacredly observed," he insisted, "the parts that are new no less than the parts that are old."[17]

A month later Tilden responded in a letter three times as long as Hayes's. He devoted more than three-quarters of the document to economic questions. In the name of reform, he denounced high taxes as draining funds from the economy, although he ignored the fact that the federal government had routinely put a portion of the revenues exceeding expenditures back into circulation by purchasing bonds and reducing the national debt. Somewhat contradictorily, he called for the retention of surplus revenues in the Treasury to help build the gold stock required for resumption, which, if necessary, could be supplemented by the sale of bonds. Echoing the essentially hard-money, orthodox tone of the St. Louis platform, he faulted the Republicans for setting a day for resumption and then not taking the necessary action to prepare for it. On the southern question, white conservatives welcomed the New Yorker's condemnation of the "insupportable misgovernment imposed upon the states of the South," and they could see little cause for concern in his meretricious promise to protect all "citizens, whatever their former condition, in every political and personal right." Tilden closed his letter with a ringing demand for civil service reform. He castigated the Republicans for countenancing "inefficiency, peculation, fraud, and malversation" and for abusing the patronage power to turn officeholders into "political mercenaries."[18]

Although "Tilden and Reform" became the hallmark of the Democrats' campaign, its effectiveness for winning votes was far from clear. The alleged wrongdoing of the Grant regime presented an easy target, but seasoned Democrats such as 1868 presidential nominee Horatio Seymour warned that "the word 'reform' is not popular with workingmen. To them it means less money spent and less work." Yet, as historian Michael F. Holt has argued, neither party in

1876 advocated a government relief program to alleviate hard times. In early August the Democratic House passed a bill to repeal the resumption clause—a move that held some appeal for inflationists in the West—but it had no chance in the Republican Senate. In effect, the essential consonance of the pro-resumption views of Hayes and Tilden rendered the question nugatory as an issue between the two major parties, leading some soft-money men to cast their lot with Peter Cooper, the Greenback Party candidate nominated on an inflationist platform. Before adjourning, the House Democrats passed a watered-down version of Blaine's schools amendment, which tended to dilute the effect of that issue in the campaign as well.[19]

It soon became clear to Hayes that the main point of difference between the parties was the southern question. On the same day he issued his letter of acceptance, white rifle clubs assaulted blacks at Hamburg, South Carolina, leaving six men dead in an attack that Grant labeled "cruel, bloodthirsty, wanton [and] unprovoked." Shortly thereafter a Senate committee investigating Mississippi reported that the Democrats had won the 1875 election and whites had "regained supremacy in the State by acts of violence, fraud, and murder, fraught with more than all the horrors of open war." These developments confirmed Hayes in his belief that any change of federal government policy in the South must hinge on continued guarantees of the rights of blacks under the Reconstruction amendments. He and other Republicans took genuine alarm at the thought of the Democrats' gaining complete control of the government in Washington, the presidency as well as Congress. Should they do so, "we shall have lively times," wrote former attorney general Edwards Pierrepont. "There will be no Negro vote except for the Confederacy one year after Tilden is President." By early August, Hayes was convinced, as he told James A. Garfield, "Our main issue must be *It is not safe to allow the Rebellion to come into power.*"[20]

Garfield and other Republican surrogates for Hayes hit these themes hard on the stump. Even Carl Schurz warned of the "continual threat" the Democrats posed to "the results of the war." "I believe in reform," Schurz told a New York audience, "but I do not believe in the reform of the rifle and the revolver in the hands of a terrorist." Republicans also warned that once in power, the Democrats would raid the Treasury to pay bogus southern claims in compensation for property destroyed or appropriated by Union forces during the war. Hayes considered the claims issue a strong argument, for "it touches the two vital things 1st the whole Rebel menace. 2d It reaches men's pockets—is an answer to 'hard times.'" The Democrats recognized the potency in the Republicans' southern issue. Tilden's close associate John Bigelow published a pamphlet denying that the governor had sympathized with slavery or with the South during the war. And two weeks before the election Tilden himself issued a letter declaring that he would veto any southern claims bills passed by Congress. Still, it remained uncertain whether the southern question could outweigh Americans' dissatisfaction with hard times. On election day, Hayes confessed that he considered "Democratic chances the best."[21]

The voters that day proved him right—at least insofar as the popular vote was concerned. Nationwide, Tilden outpolled Hayes by a quarter of a million votes, finishing with 51 percent of the total to 48 percent for Hayes. The electoral vote count told another story, however. Tilden won eight states of the old Confederacy, along with the border states of Delaware, Maryland, Kentucky, Missouri, and West Virginia, plus four swing states in the North: New York, Indiana, Connecticut, and New Jersey, for a total of 184. Hayes took all the other states of the North and the West, for a total of 166. But both parties claimed 19 votes from South Carolina, Florida, and Louisiana, the last three Reconstruction states still in Republican hands. (The Democrats also claimed a single vote in Oregon on a technicality, but the ensuing controversy focused primarily on the three southern states.) Both President Grant and the Democratic Party leaders dispatched "visiting statesmen" to the three disputed states to observe the vote count, and in the end both slates of electors sent their ballots to Washington to be counted.

Then what? The Constitution was vague regarding the process, stating simply that at a joint session of Congress the president of the Senate should "open all the certificates and the votes shall then be counted." But who should "count" the votes? The current Senate president was a Republican, Thomas Ferry, and many members of his party thought that he held indisputable power to tally the electoral votes. Democrats argued that the requirement of a joint session mandated participation by both houses, the Democratic House as well as the Republican Senate. Tilden's hopes seemed to lie in a deadlock, or the failure of either man to receive a majority of the electoral vote, which, under the Constitution, would throw the decision into the House, where the majority Democrats would choose him over Hayes. But could the Democrats make such a move stick? Besides the Senate, the Republicans controlled the presidency and, therefore, the armed forces. In addition, should the case evolve into a legal dispute, Republican justices formed a clear majority on the Supreme Court. Should the Democrats attempt such a step, Ferry could proceed to the count in Hayes's favor, supported by the other branches of the government. Indeed, this was the Republicans' ace in the hole throughout the controversy.

But some Republicans in Congress had doubts about Ferry's prerogative, and others feared that brazen steamroller tactics to win this struggle would flatten Republican prospects for years to come. These men were open to suggestions for the creation of some sort of ad hoc tribunal to resolve the controversy, a gambit that many Democrats saw as offering the only realistic hope of putting Tilden in office. In mid-January 1877, special House and Senate committees devised a bill to create a fifteen-member electoral commission to decide which electoral ballots to count. The members would include five senators, five representatives, and four Supreme Court justices who would choose a fifth justice. It was presumed that the members from Congress and the four justices would be evenly balanced between the parties. Democrats found the scheme especially palatable when it appeared that the fifth justice would be David Davis, a political independent. Republicans, in turn, found it more agreeable when Davis, after his election to the Senate from Illinois, disqualified himself from service on the commission. Still, 90 percent of the Democrats backed the bill on its final passage, while fewer than 40 percent of the Republicans did. After Davis's withdrawal, the remaining eligible justices were all Republicans, and Joseph P. Bradley of New Jersey took the seat.

On February 9 Bradley joined his fellow Republicans in awarding Florida to Hayes, a decision that set the pattern for the commission's subsequent deliberations. Democrats expressed outrage, and some in the House resorted to obstructionist tactics to delay the commission's report on the electoral count in order to block Hayes's election. These tactics gave rise to the assertion in some historical accounts that southern Democrats struck a deal with representatives of Hayes whereby southerners in the House would move to get the count completed and let Hayes win, in exchange for promises from the Republicans that Hayes, as president, would remove the remaining federal troops from the last two southern states under Republican rule, Louisiana and South Carolina, and thereby permit the Democrats to take control. Additionally, according to some versions of the story, Hayes would push for federal expenditures for internal improvements in the South. Behind-the-scenes conversations certainly did occur, but in fact they had little impact on the outcome of the crisis.

In the first place, it was southerners who clung to obstructionism in the House, while northern Democrats were more likely to favor letting the count go forward. In reality, the obstructionism was essentially toothless and had scant prospect of denying Hayes the presidency. Again, the Republicans' control of the Senate, the presidency (and the army), and the Supreme Court meant that Tilden and

HARPER'S WEEKLY.
JOURNAL OF CIVILIZATION

Vol. XXI.—No. 1056.]   NEW YORK, SATURDAY, MARCH 24, 1877.   [WITH A SUPPLEMENT. PRICE TEN CENTS.

Entered according to Act of Congress, in the Year 1877, by Harper & Brothers, in the Office of the Librarian of Congress, at Washington.

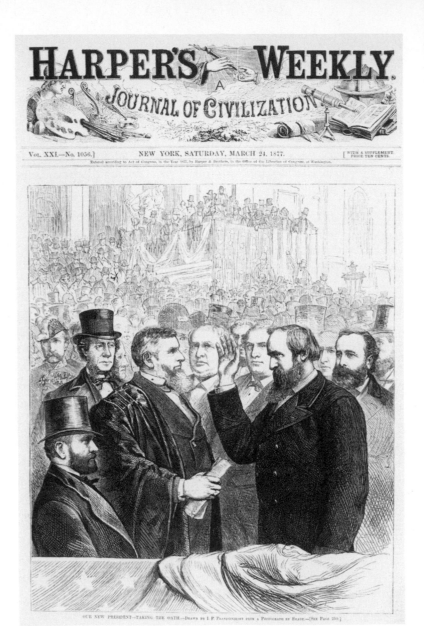

OUR NEW PRESIDENT—TAKING THE OATH.—DRAWN BY I. P. PRANISHNIKOFF FROM A PHOTOGRAPH BY BRADY.—[SEE PAGE 230.]

President Rutherford B. Hayes takes the oath of office while a pensive Ulysses S. Grant, at left, looks on. (*Harper's Weekly*, March 24, 1877)

the Democrats could find no effective recourse in congressional action, force, or litigation. At any time, the Republican president of the Senate could simply pronounce Hayes the winner. Moreover, during his campaign Hayes had signaled his willingness to see local self-government restored in the South and was not pushed to that position by an empty threat to deny him the presidency. But Hayes had always insisted that such a policy of withdrawal depended on the southerners' pledge to uphold the Reconstruction Amendments. In their key meeting with southerners in Washington, Hayes's allies held the upper hand. Rather than cravenly offering southerners withdrawal of the troops to gain the presidency, the Hayes people demanded specific guarantees from representatives of Louisiana and South Carolina that the rights of African Americans would be upheld. The count proceeded slowly but inexorably, and shortly before inauguration day, Hayes emerged as the victor.

Once in the White House, Hayes did not remove the troops immediately. He required further and more public promises from the Democratic leaders of Louisiana and South Carolina before issuing the withdrawal orders. In a broader sense, Hayes hoped that a new southern policy would help achieve reconciliation between the races and between the sections. He appointed a former Confederate general to his cabinet, and within the South he granted patronage favors to Democrats who showed themselves amenable to a new course. Early in his term he took a goodwill tour through the South, where citizens greeted him warmly as an apostle of reunion. On the political level, Hayes sought to divide the South on issues other than race and broaden the scope of the Republican Party in the region by appealing to southerners, especially former Whigs, who subscribed to many of the Republicans' economic policies. "He expects some reverses at first," noted one observer, "but thinks the leaven will work and that the barriers of vice, ignorance, and hatred will be overcome."[22]

It soon became clear, however, that Hayes's objectives were unrealistic. Southern leaders had no intention of keeping their promises to protect blacks' rights. White southerners continued to regard the Republican Party as synonymous with the "horrors" of Reconstruction and black rule. In off-year elections in the fall of 1877, Republicans in Virginia saw their 40 percent share of the vote in 1876 fall to 4.1 percent, and in Mississippi their vote declined from 30 percent to 1.2 percent. These results confirmed the criticism that many men within Hayes's own party had leveled against his southern policy. Substantial numbers of Republicans believed that the president had abandoned blacks' rights and wrecked the southern wing of the party.

Hayes also angered some fellow Republicans by his efforts toward civil service reform, which he had promised in his campaign. A few months after taking office, he issued an order barring federal officeholders from managing political organizations or campaigns and banning the involuntary assessment of part of their salaries for party coffers. When the collector of customs in New York, Chester Arthur, resisted these new rules, Hayes fired him, thereby incurring the wrath of the New York Republican machine headed by Senator Roscoe Conkling. Only after a fierce struggle in the Senate did the president succeed in getting Arthur's successor confirmed. In this fight Hayes was motivated not merely by reform impulses but also by factional animosity against Conkling. Moreover, during election seasons, administration officials gave a loose interpretation to Hayes's civil service order and permitted officeholders to campaign and make voluntary political contributions. Nonetheless, party cadres bridled at Hayes's policy, and Congress refused to enact his proposals into law.

Democrats could reasonably expect to profit from divisions among Republicans over Hayes's southern and civil service policies, but an investigation of alleged fraud in the election of 1876 launched by House Democrats in the spring of 1878 helped reunite the GOP. Republicans rallied to a defense of the president's title to office and decried the House committee's inquiry as threatening revolution.

Indeed, the reaction against the move was so strong that within a month, large numbers of House Democrats joined the Republicans in declaring that neither Congress nor the courts could reverse the 1876 outcome. The investigation proceeded anyway and backfired against the Democrats with the discovery of the so-called cipher despatches, which implicated Tilden aides in bribery attempts during the election controversy.

In the midterm congressional election campaign in 1878, many Republicans, including Hayes, believed that they should put the southern question aside and focus instead on the currency issue. Hard times lingered, and popular discontent had occasionally burst forth in incidents such as the Great Railway Strike of 1877. Many Americans still saw inflation as a cure for economic stagnation, but Hayes stood firm for financial orthodoxy. Early in 1878 his allies in Congress blocked a measure for free coinage of silver, but the House and Senate overrode his veto of the Bland-Allison bill, which called for a limited remonetization of the white metal. Determined to proceed with specie payment for the greenbacks, Hayes skirted his civil service principles and used patronage leverage to secure defeat of an inflationist attempt to repeal the Resumption Act.

Hayes looked for vindication of his administration in the 1878 elections and believed that a unified GOP canvass based on the money question could eclipse internal party criticisms of his southern and civil service policies. He told Republicans that the issue of "a sound Constitutional Currency is the most important question now before the Country," and he urged them to "sink all other Controversies."[23] In some measure, Hayes's proposed emphasis for the campaign foreshadowed the primacy that economic issues would achieve by the end of the century. The president himself took extended speaking tours through the Midwest and the South, arguing that a sound currency was indispensable to prosperity. Other party speakers followed suit, portraying the GOP as the champion of moral money and condemning the Democratic Party as unsound and no better than the Greenback

Party on the issue. These shafts were well aimed, for in many states the Democrats called for repeal of the Resumption Act and generally vied with the Greenbackers for inflationist support.

The results in the 1878 elections, in the North at least, justified the Republicans' course. In state contests, the GOP carried New York, Pennsylvania, Illinois, and Ohio, as well as several smaller states. Outside the former slave states, the party gained three seats in the national House. Hayes ascribed the outcome to the money question and saw it as "a verdict in favor of maintaining unstained the national credit." Similarly, James A. Garfield thought the result gave "an immense impulse to business by adding confidence to the sanctity of the public faith." Indeed, Garfield believed, "this election changes the face of the political sky." Two months after the election, the Treasury successfully resumed specie payments for greenbacks, as mandated by the 1875 law.[24]

Yet during and after the campaign, some GOP leaders opposed the shift in emphasis to the currency issue from the defense of civil rights for southern African Americans. The chairman of the GOP Congressional Campaign Committee complained that the party was "play[ing] the comedy of the Almighty Dollar throughout the summer and fall" while failing to remind "the North of the suppression of the Republican vote of the South." Violence and intimidation of blacks in several southern states underscored such complaints and prompted Justice Department officials to instruct federal officials to enforce the election laws vigorously. After the election, Hayes himself conceded that in Louisiana, South Carolina, and elsewhere, blacks had been denied the right to vote "by state legislation, by frauds, by intimidation, and by violence of the most atrocious character." Although he was reluctant to admit it, his conciliatory policy had failed, as was clear from the election results in the South. In the new Congress, the seventy-three representatives chosen from the former Confederate states included only three Republicans. No southern Republican won a seat in the Senate, where the party's

HARPER'S WEEKLY.

A JOURNAL OF CIVILIZATION

Vol. XXIII.—No. 1164.]   NEW YORK, SATURDAY, APRIL 19, 1879.   [WITH A SUPPLEMENT. PRICE TEN CENTS.

Entered according to Act of Congress, in the Year 1879, by Harper & Brothers, in the Office of the Librarian of Congress, at Washington.

With his gun and knife planted on his chamber desk, a southern congressman rummages through his bag of demands from the Solid South. (*Harper's Weekly*, April 19, 1879)

representation from the region fell from six to two. This decline contributed to Republicans' loss of their majority in the upper chamber
for the first time since the war. For the remainder of his term Hayes
confronted a Democratic majority in both houses of Congress.[25]

Democrats' behavior in the new Congress demonstrated the continued salience of the southern question. On several occasions they
sought to roll back the voting rights legislation from the early years of
Reconstruction by attaching repeal provisions to routine appropriations bills. Hayes condemned such riders as "coercive dictation." He
repeatedly vetoed these spending bills and allowed portions of the
government to go unfunded rather than accept the undoing of federal
laws for enforcing the right to vote. In the minds of Republicans, this
rider controversy underscored what Garfield labeled "the wicked
spirit of the Democratic party, especially the Southern wing of it." It
also confirmed the crucial importance Republicans in 1876 had assigned to retaining control of at least one branch of the government.
Galvanized anew for the state elections of 1879, GOP conventions in
several states applauded Hayes for vetoing the riders and censured
the Democrats for reviving sectional animosity. In addition, the Republicans reprised their defense of a sound currency and won a
sweeping victory throughout the North.[26]

In considerable measure, the Republicans owed their triumph to
an upturn in the economy that had begun in 1878 and was in full
swing by the fall of 1879. Naturally they cited the recovery as evidence of their successful currency policies. Over the years the Republicans had achieved what appeared to be a workable settlement
of the money question, which included resumption of specie payments, the continued use of greenbacks and national banknotes, and
the remonetization of silver limited enough to preserve the gold standard. Although hard- and soft-money advocates still differed about
what further measures might be necessary, the urge to leave well
enough alone moved increasing numbers of Republicans to stand by
the monetary system that had emerged.

As Hayes entered his fourth year in office, both the country and his party were in such condition that he could reasonably expect reelection in 1880. In 1876, however, he had avowed that he would serve only one term, and he stuck by that determination. Having assumed the presidency under a cloud, Hayes would join that small group of presidents who have left the White House more popular than when they went in. Even so, many in his party had balked at his policies, especially his southern policy, and the race for the presidential nomination in 1880 held the potential to reorient the party's direction. For the Democrats, meanwhile, the Hayes years had solidified their grip on the South, and the challenge they faced was to extend their appeal beyond that formidable bastion. Each party would now search for effective ways to break the partisan equilibrium that had come to define the nation's political life.

THREE

"Fold Up the Bloody Shirt"

Despite the GOP's strong showing in the elections of 1879, factionalism plagued the Republicans as they approached the election of
1880. The race for the party's presidential nomination turned into a
fierce contest that was not only a clash of personalities but a struggle
over the party's ideological direction. The Democrats, for their part,
hoped to retain their hold on Congress and vindicate their loss in
1876 in the race for the White House. Yet the Democrats continued
to attack the voting rights laws through riders well into the spring of
1880, an effort hardly calculated to broaden their appeal beyond the
Solid South. Indeed, their assault played directly into the hands of
Republicans who sought to make the southern question the centerpiece of their 1880 campaign.

For those Republicans, former president Ulysses S. Grant emerged
as the ideal "strong man" to bring the party back to its true faith
after the apostasy and weakness of the Hayes years. "If the constitutional rights of citizens are invaded," Grant's former Treasury secretary George S. Boutwell insisted, "he will employ every constitutional
power for their protection." Moreover, Grant appealed to Republicans who disdained Hayes's civil service policies as subverting
party fealty and undermining the party's best interests. Known as
Stalwarts, these Republicans looked to Grant to reinvigorate the

party's faithful and reestablish its principles after years of supposed drifting under "Miss Nancy Jane Hayes."[1]

After leaving the White House, Grant and his wife had set off on a round-the-world tour that lasted more than two years. The enthusiastic acclaim showered on him by parliaments and potentates made the former president a citizen of the world and served to eclipse memories back home of the troubled moments during his eight years in the White House. Now, said supporters, in a compliment unwittingly backhanded, Grant was ready to be president. When the general returned to the West Coast of the United States in the fall of 1879, the cheering continued as he traveled eastward from fete to fete.

But some observers believed that Grant had returned home too early and that his supporters would find it difficult to maintain the popular fervor until the Republican convention in June. Certainly he would have no walkover, for other imposing candidates soon entered the field. Hayes made no overt effort to tap a successor, but Secretary of the Treasury John Sherman emerged as the candidate most able and willing to vindicate the administration and its policies. Although Sherman defended Hayes's southern policy while also calling for the full protection of citizens' rights, the central thrust of his candidacy was to turn voters' attention to economic questions. Sherman had first entered Congress in 1855 and had chaired both the Ways and Means Committee in the House and the Finance Committee in the Senate. He had long been regarded as the GOP's leading expert on economic matters, but he had made a good many enemies within the party over the years, especially in pivotal New York, where Stalwart Republicans fingered the secretary as their chief nemesis in their patronage battles with the administration. Indeed, New York senator Roscoe Conkling was the driving force behind Grant's bid for another term.

More formidable than Sherman was James G. Blaine, who had narrowly lost the nomination to Hayes in 1876. Now representing Maine in the Senate, Blaine had long served as an indefatigable campaigner for Republicans around the country, and despite the Mulligan revelations of 1876, he enjoyed great esteem in many quarters of the party. A bitter enemy of Conkling since the days when they had clashed in Congress more than a decade before, Blaine thought a new Grant presidency would not only be a front for the New Yorker and his Stalwart allies, it would also take the party and the country backward rather than forward. Blaine stood at the head of the anti-Stalwart faction known as Half-Breeds. Although he had on occasion proved to be a fearsome foe of the Democrats in debate over the southern question, Blaine, like Sherman, strove to move the GOP's emphasis to economic issues. He and other Half-Breeds, while not dismissing questions of section and race altogether, believed that the party's future success lay in making appeals primarily to voters' pocketbook concerns.

When Republicans arrived for their national convention in Chicago, many had come directly from Congress, where they had battled with the Democrats in the riders controversy. They issued a platform with a strongly worded civil rights plank, insisting that "honest voters must be protected against terrorism, violence, or fraud."[2] This sentiment seemed to resonate with the call for Grant, who entered the convention with the largest number of delegates, slightly ahead of Blaine but less than a majority. On the first ballot, Grant posted 304 votes to Blaine's 284, with Sherman coming in a distant third with 93. The voting showed little change for more than thirty ballots, and Sherman's chances rested on the prospect that the enduring deadlock would turn the frustrated delegates his way. Instead, on the thirty-fourth ballot, Wisconsin, which had previously divided its vote, threw its support to Sherman's floor manager, James A. Garfield, a longtime congressman known as a friend of Blaine. With Indiana following suit on the next tally, the rush was on, and on the thirty-sixth ballot, the dark horse Garfield won the nomination. An immovable 306 delegates stood by Grant to the end, and in an effort to reconcile the warring factions, the convention gave the vice presidential spot to New Yorker Chester A. Arthur, the Stalwart former collector of customs fired by Hayes.

In addition to the lengthy plank on the southern question, the platform gave credit to the GOP for the return of prosperity. The party had not only brought the greenbacks up to par with gold but had also "given us a currency absolutely good and equal in every part of our extended country." The Republicans took credit for reducing the national debt, increasing veterans' pensions, and creating a large, favorable balance of trade. The platform gave only brief mention to the tariff issue, avowing that "the duties levied for the purpose of revenue should so discriminate as to favor American labor." On social issues, it called for limits on Chinese immigration, a ban on the use of public funds for sectarian education, and the elimination of polygamy, which Mormons were practicing in Utah Territory.[3]

Despite his status as a dark horse nominee, Garfield enjoyed a national reputation. A member of Congress since 1863, he had rapidly risen to the chairmanship of the powerful Appropriations Committee, and after Blaine had left the House, the Ohioan won general recognition as the Republicans' leader on the floor. He held moderate views on the South, tilted toward civil service reform, and stood adamantly in the forefront of the party's hard-money forces. Robust and forty-nine years old, he seemed in his prime to take command of the Republican Party and the country.

On the Democratic side, the putative front-runner for the presidential nomination projected just the opposite sort of image. Hordes of Democrats favored the "reelection" of Samuel J. Tilden in 1880, but his age, sixty-six, and his frail health after a mild stroke cast doubt on his capacity to mount an effective campaign or to run the government. Nor were his prospects helped by the deep and abiding enmity of Tammany Hall, which could cost him the vote of critical New York State. Nonetheless, sentimental attachment kept Tilden's name in play until he finally withdrew on the eve of the national convention.

Throughout the spring, other men jockeyed to inherit Tilden's support, but the Democratic tradition of state and local orientation left the party with a dearth of men of truly national reputation. House Speaker Samuel J. Randall came the closest, but his protectionist tariff views, geared to the needs of business and labor in his industrial Philadelphia congressional district, won him few friends among the predominantly low-tariff Democrats of the West and South. Hoosier Thomas A. Hendricks, Tilden's old running mate, could not generate support much beyond the bounds of his own state. Delaware's Thomas F. Bayard had eloquently expounded Democratic doctrine on the Senate floor for years, but he lacked flair, and his pro-southern pronouncements during the secession crisis of 1861 would play into Republican hands in a "bloody shirt" campaign.

If the southern question was going to dominate the campaign, a growing number of Democrats saw the nomination of Union general Winfield Scott Hancock as a way to defuse the issue in the North. A career army man, Hancock had distinguished himself in the war, especially at Gettysburg. During Reconstruction, as military commander of Louisiana and Texas, the conservative Hancock fell in with the policies of President Andrew Johnson and thereby won the undying affection of many southern Democrats. Possessing no political record to invite embarrassing scrutiny, and unburdened by enemies within the otherwise discordant party, Hancock gained support as a candidate whom all factions could live with and fight for. Having shelved Randall, the Democrats of Pennsylvania championed the general at the national convention, where he was the clear favorite of the crowds in the galleries. On the second ballot, Hancock won the nomination. For vice president, the convention tapped former Indiana congressman William H. English, whose large personal wealth, party managers hoped, could help the Democrats capture his doubtful home state.

The platform stated that the "right to a free ballot" should be "maintained in every part" of the country, but it also denounced "centralization" and called for "home rule," code words for continued white dominance in the South. Indeed, the party's real intentions regarding voting rights were more truly captured by South Carolina governor Wade Hampton's "pledge" to the convention that the "solid South" would do whatever was necessary to deliver "its solid vote" for Hancock. In their platform, the Democrats, like the Republicans, opposed Chinese immigration. On the schools question, the platform laconically favored "separation of Church and State, for the good of each; common schools fostered and protected." On the tariff issue, the Democrats uttered just five words, "a tariff for revenue only," thereby opening themselves to charges of indifference to the protection of American producers from foreign competition. Monetary conservatives secured a plank endorsing "honest money, consisting of gold and silver, and paper convertible into coin on demand." This apparent acceptance of the financial settlement achieved in the late 1870s suggested that the currency issue would play a secondary role in the fall campaign.[4]

Americans dissatisfied with that settlement could turn to the Greenback Party, which nominated Iowa congressman James B. Weaver for president. That party's convention called for the abolition of national banks, the substitution of greenbacks for national banknotes, and the unlimited coinage of silver. The return of prosperity had diminished the appeal of this sort of inflationism, however, and GOP speakers eagerly portrayed the Democrats as just as dangerously inimical to sound money as the Greenbackers. In the face of Democratic professions of monetary orthodoxy, some Republicans were content to see Greenbackers in the field draining inflationist voters away from the Democrats. Indeed, in some closely contested congressional races, the GOP helped underwrite the Greenbackers.

In general, the Republicans were in fighting trim. After spending some time licking their wounds after the national convention,

Grant and Conkling both campaigned for the ticket. At the outset, Republicans prepared to make the southern question the center of their campaign, in response to the South's persistent recalcitrance as embodied in the rider controversy in Congress and as illustrated by Hampton's defiance at the Democratic convention. Even Hayes endorsed the strategy: "The failure of the South to faithfully observe the Fifteenth Amendment is the cause of the failure of all efforts towards complete pacification. It is on this hook that the bloody shirt now hangs." Campaign speakers stressed the issue, and it formed the subject of twelve of the nineteen issue chapters in the party's campaign textbook.[5]

In response, the Democrats extolled Hancock's illustrious war record and his unquestionable loyalty. In his letter of acceptance, the general stated emphatically that the Thirteenth, Fourteenth, and Fifteenth amendments were "inviolable," and he promised to "resist with all of my power any attempt to impair or evade the full force and effect of the Constitution." On other issues, Hancock said virtually nothing beyond a call for "practical civil service reform" and "a sedulous and scrupulous care of the public credit."[6] Given Hancock's background, the Democrats were hard-pressed to praise his civilian record, which was nonexistent, or to tout his positions on the issues, which were vague if not incoherent. Hence, Democrats spent much of their energy attacking Garfield's integrity, alleging, among other things, that as a congressman, he had profited in the Crédit Mobilier scandal.

Both camps looked to the September state elections in Maine for some sign regarding the strength of their appeals. In the gubernatorial race, the Democratic-Greenbacker fusion candidate won by one-tenth of a percent, with the Republicans losing the popular vote for governor for the first time since the party's founding in the 1850s. Although the GOP won a majority in the legislature, party strategists were shocked, and they pored over the returns for some guidance for the remainder of the campaign. Maine's economy had not yet recovered, and Garfield and others noted that the party had run well in manufacturing towns but had lost in shipping towns. That result pointed to the effectiveness of the Republicans' stand on the tariff. Party campaigners had routinely championed protectionism, especially for labor, but Garfield and other leaders now pushed to make the issue the centerpiece of their campaign. According to one story, perhaps apocryphal, Blaine commanded workers at party headquarters to "fold up the bloody shirt" and "shift the main issue to protection."[7] Republicans by no means dropped the southern question, but they did give new emphasis to the tariff. In campaign speeches and a blizzard of pamphlets, Republicans and their allies in business warned that the Democrats' notions of "a tariff for revenue only" imperiled the fragile recovery after the long depression of the 1870s. Linking sectional and economic issues, the GOP charged that the Democrats' low-tariff views, for decades the position of the South on the issue, simply represented the continued subservience of the Democratic Party to its dominant southern wing.

Highlighting economic issues rendered Hancock's wartime service less relevant and allowed Republicans to accentuate his deficient understanding of civil government. Hancock helped them when he stated in a newspaper interview that the "tariff question is a local question" with which "the general government seldom cares to interfere." Although the general no doubt meant to say that tariff duties on particular items were of keenest interest to the localities that produced them, the Republicans sent up a howl at this sign of his tenuous grasp of public policy. Hancock quickly moved to repair the damage by asserting that he was "too sound an American to advocate any departure from the general features of a policy that has been largely instrumental in building up our industries and keeping Americans from the competition of the underpaid labor of Europe." This statement merely confirmed the issue's prominence; it convinced few that Hancock could outstrip the GOP's protectionism or withstand the low-tariff orthodoxy of the southern-dominated Democratic Party.[8]

Toward the end of the campaign the Democrats sought to undercut the Republicans' tariff appeals to workers by releasing the text of a letter Garfield had allegedly written condoning the immigration of cheap Chinese labor. It was a clumsy forgery, but Democratic newspapers and speakers played it for all it was worth. Appearing near the end of the campaign, the forgery may have had some impact. On election day, Hancock ran well in the Far West, narrowly losing Oregon and becoming the first Democrat since 1856 to carry California and the first ever to win Nevada.

Otherwise, however, the outcome confirmed the nation's enduring sectional division. Hancock won every former slave state plus New Jersey, while Garfield won everywhere else, including the key doubtful states of New York and Indiana. Nationwide, Garfield ran ahead of Hancock by fewer than 10,000 votes out of more than 9 million, and he took the electoral vote by 214 to 155. The Greenbacker James Weaver garnered 306,000 votes, or 3.3 percent of the total. Republicans won control of the House of Representatives and would be tied with the Democrats in the new Senate.

With the result so close, no one could say with certainty whether sectional or economic issues had exerted the greater influence. Garfield concluded that both "the distrust of the Solid South and of adverse financial legislation have been the chief factors."[9] The new president had scant time to formulate policies on either front, however. After six months in office he succumbed to an assassin's bullet. The most notable achievement of his brief term came in a titanic struggle over patronage when Roscoe Conkling attempted to block Garfield's Half-Breed appointee for collector of customs at New York. In the end, Garfield triumphed and essentially drove Conkling out of politics.

It was supremely ironic, then, that Conkling's former ally, Chester Arthur, ascended to the presidency after Garfield's death, in September 1881. As a quartermaster general during the Civil War, Arthur had exhibited clear talents for organization. After the war, he applied those skills on behalf of the New York Republican machine, managing the spoils-rich U.S. Custom House from 1871 until he was dismissed by Hayes in 1879. Though well educated and cultivated, Arthur did not shun the low arts of politics, and he showed particular proficiency at squeezing party contributions out of federal workers and channeling the money into election campaigns.

As if the new president's tainted reputation as a spoilsman were not burdensome enough, the circumstances of his succession made his entry into the White House even less auspicious. At the time of the shooting, Garfield's assassin, Charles Guiteau, had declared, "I am a Stalwart, and Arthur will be president."[10] Guiteau was clearly insane, but he had also desperately sought an appointment in the new administration. After his crime he was labeled a disappointed office seeker whose hideous act represented the ultimate barbarity wrought by the evil practice of spoils. The assassination spurred the efforts of reformers, who also portrayed a revamping of the system of appointments as necessary to meet the needs of a modernizing society. Less than three months after taking office, a chastened Arthur devoted a section of his first annual message to a mild endorsement of reform in the civil service.

But, like other politicians, Arthur was well aware of the potential influence the patronage held for achieving policy ends. In his approach to the southern question, he used appointments to reward independent Democratic groups challenging the hegemony of Bourbon Democrats in the region. This movement met with some success, but it came no closer than Hayes's effort to break the Solid South, and it wound up alienating some African Americans and white southern Republicans. Arthur advocated aid to education as a means of uplifting poor blacks in the South, and after the Supreme Court struck down the Civil Rights Act of 1875, he called for new legislation to secure the equal enjoyment of constitutional rights. Neither proposal, however, made it through Congress. Following an established pattern, Justice Department efforts to protect the right to vote met with scant success because of the reluctance of southern juries to convict violators of the federal election laws.

In economic matters, the currency question remained relatively quiescent during the Arthur years. With the return of prosperity, another condition arose to capture the attention of politicians. Good times led to mounting tax collections that swelled the government's coffers, so that by 1882 the federal budgetary surplus had climbed to $145 million, more than a third of the government's total revenue. How to deal with this bounty became an important issue, and in seeking a solution, Arthur was at odds with Republican opinion in Congress.

Many activist-minded Republicans had come around to the view that the rapid changes in American society justified applying the burgeoning revenues to the needs of the industrializing economy. In the summer of 1882 Congress passed a record-breaking Rivers and Harbors bill, as the annual omnibus internal improvements legislation was commonly called. At $19 million, the price tag seems modest by modern standards, but at the time it was unprecedented, representing a 64 percent increase over the previous year's bill.

Arthur vetoed it. Although he favored some of the bill's provisions, he considered others unconstitutional because they funded purely local projects. More broadly, he warned that "extravagant expenditure of public money" would have a "demoralizing effect." Among the press and the public, the president won a chorus of praise for his stand, but within twenty-four hours a bipartisan vote in Congress overrode his veto. In the face of the bill's unpopularity, its defenders exhibited courage at the risk of political censure. One of its supporters, Massachusetts senator George F. Hoar, came in for withering criticism but nonetheless insisted that "there should be some things to which the whole people of the United States shall accustom themselves to look to the General Government as a benefactor."[11]

Besides increased spending, the other way to trim the surplus was to reduce the revenue, and this too led to controversy. Historically, tariff duties had provided the bulk of federal tax receipts; in the 1880s they typically yielded 60 percent or more of the total. Internal levies applied primarily to alcohol and tobacco, and members of Congress shied away from the political hazard in reducing these "sin taxes." But revising the tariff also invited political repercussions among affected interests, and growing numbers in both parties saw the creation of an expert commission to investigate the tariff as a way to minimize the risk. In 1880 a bipartisan majority in the Senate had passed a proposal for such a body, but it had failed in the House. In his first annual message, in December 1881, Arthur endorsed the idea. The president asserted that the tariff laws "need revision," though he insisted that American interests required that "important changes should be made with caution."[12] If Congress could not resolve the issue, he said, it should authorize a commission. Recognizing the drift of sentiment and moving to control the process, Republican protectionists quickly introduced legislation for a commission, and the bill passed during the spring of 1882. The nine members appointed by Arthur showed a decidedly protectionist tinge. The group traveled widely for three months, taking voluminous testimony, mostly from representatives of special interests who volunteered to appear before the body.

With its report due in December 1882, the commission pursued its work against the backdrop of the midterm congressional election campaign. During the canvass the Democrats condemned the Republicans for extravagance, abuse of the patronage for political ends, and failure to take action to reform the civil service or revise the tariff. Moreover, the campaign showed that Arthur had not succeeded in unifying the Republican Party behind his leadership. The circumstances of his coming to power foreclosed any attempt by the president to swing administration patronage to his old friends in the Stalwart faction, and many of them bristled at the neglect. On the other hand, Blaine, who had served as Garfield's secretary of state and resigned soon after his death, chafed at the new administration's abandonment of some of his foreign policy initiatives. Many of Blaine's Half-Breed followers shared his sense of alienation. Nor did civil service reformers warm to the ascendancy of the old "spoilsman" Arthur. Adding to the growing discontent, the administration's clumsy intervention to secure the New York gubernatorial nomination for Secretary of the Treasury Charles J. Folger offended many Republicans, not only in the Empire State but elsewhere as well. Folger lost in a landslide to Democrat Grover Cleveland, a relative novice in the state's politics. Republicans in general did poorly in the 1882 elections. They saw their majority in the national House of Representatives swing to Democratic control by almost two to one, although the GOP would have a slender margin of four seats in the new Senate.

The election outcome spurred the Republicans to make the most of the lame-duck session of the outgoing Forty-seventh Congress, which would run from December 1882 to March 1883. In his annual message on the session's first day, Arthur stepped up his support for pending civil service legislation, citing the people's "earnest wish for prompt and definitive action." As the government had grown larger and more complex, he argued, it had "outgrown" the old system of "personal direction of appointments to the civil service."[13] In January 1883 Congress passed the Pendleton Civil Service Act by bipartisan majorities in both houses. The act established a Civil Service Commission, mandated competitive examinations for appointment to classified federal offices, barred congressional recommendations regarding appointments, and protected federal workers from political assessments. As an unintended consequence, this last provision fueled the parties' reliance on special interests for financial support. The law originally applied to only 15 percent of the federal workforce, but later presidents broadened its coverage. Despite its initial limited scope, the Pendleton Act proved to be an irreversible step toward a merit system in federal employment. It was not without irony that Arthur, known for most of his previous career as a competent administrator but nonetheless a spoilsman, signed the Pendleton Act of 1883, the most significant reform in the civil service enacted in the nineteenth century.

The outcome of the 1882 elections impelled Republicans to take action on the tariff as well. At the opening of Congress, the Tariff Commission sparked surprise by recommending reductions in customs duties of 20 to 25 percent. At the same time, Arthur weighed in with his judgment that "the present tariff system is in many respects unjust" and "large reductions from the customs revenue are entirely feasible." The secretary of the Treasury also called for "substantial reductions."[14] Both houses of Congress spent enormous amounts of time deliberating the issue and came under great pressure from interests unhappy with the recommendations of the commission and the administration. Although exceptions appeared on both sides of the aisle, Republicans generally labored to salvage as much of the protective system as possible, while Democrats pushed for lower duties. The question was complicated by the self-serving willingness of manufacturing interests to see the customs duties on the raw materials they purchased fall more steeply than the duties on their own finished products.

As the session wore on and the prospect of a resolution seemed dim, the administration floated the rumor that if no bill passed, Arthur would call the new Congress, dominated by Democrats in the House, into special session to deal with the issue. This signal tended to confirm the suspicion of some protectionists that the president was at heart "in the hands of Free-Traders."[15] After a series of complicated maneuvers, Congress finally approved a measure that raised some duties and reduced others but overall produced an average rate only slightly lower than previous legislation. Although this outcome met criticism on many fronts, the act drew the harshest rebuke from the producers of raw materials, who felt that it tilted toward the interests of manufacturers. Among the most aggrieved were sheep farmers, angered that duties on wool were cut far more than the duties on woolens. Dubbed the Mongrel Tariff, this legislation in the spring of 1883 ensured that the issue would play an important role in the next year's presidential election campaign.

Among the aspirants for the Republican presidential nomination in 1884 was John Sherman, senator from Ohio, where state elections in 1883 would provide a test of the new tariff act's political impact. Although Sherman was not on the ballot, which included only state and local offices, the tariff issue loomed large in the contest. As a leading member of the Senate Finance Committee, Sherman came in for severe criticism from the farmers of Ohio, one of the nation's leading wool-producing states. Buckeye Democrats flooded the state with pamphlets accusing Sherman and other Republicans of "fleecing the flockmasters" through "tariff tinkering" that cost Ohio wool growers $6 million. Sherman denounced the Democrats' allegations as "the sheerest piece of hypocrisy," insisting that a majority of Republican senators, including himself, had voted to retain a higher duty on wool while all but three Democrats plus a handful of New England Republicans had voted against it. Even so, in the fall election, the Democratic state ticket prevailed in Ohio, and the party won a majority in both houses of the legislature. In addition to the tariff issue, a prohibition measure sponsored by Republicans in the state legislature had driven thousands of German Americans from the GOP. A wool grower who had remained loyal to Sherman sent his condolences on the outcome and assured the senator that with the "wool tariff restored we can carry Ohio for a republican President." Yet with Congress now split between a Democratic House and a Republican Senate, efforts to enact any new tariff legislation stood virtually no chance.[16]

As the presidential nomination season approached, Sherman could not count on the united support even of his own state, and he failed to gain much traction. Despite his incumbency, President Arthur's prospects were far from auspicious. As president, he had risen above the doubts bred by his background and had shown himself to be a competent if low-key administrator. Yet he could hardly claim to be even the titular head of his party; many Stalwarts and virtually all the Half-Breeds and reformers remained alienated. Moreover,

Arthur's health had deteriorated in the White House. He was diagnosed with Bright's disease, a kidney ailment usually fatal, but he kept the condition a secret so as not to alarm the country or political allies working on his behalf. (Arthur succumbed to the illness in November 1886).

How much Arthur truly desired the nomination remains a matter of speculation, although he did not halt his supporters' earnest efforts. Their greatest source of strength was in the "rotten boroughs" of the South, where federal officeholders who were linked to the administration formed the core of the Republican Party. To a lesser degree, administration men secured delegates elsewhere, although in New York, the president's home state, they managed to win less than half the delegation. Arthur was popular among many businessmen, particularly merchants, as evinced two weeks before the national convention by a huge rally at New York's Cooper Union addressed by former Treasury secretary Benjamin Bristow and religious leader Henry Ward Beecher. Yet a rash of bank failures and a collapse in stock prices in May cast some doubt on Arthur's and the Republicans' stewardship of the economy. But even though he was handicapped, the president remained in the race. Whether or not he believed that his health would allow him to perform his duties for another term, he could view a nomination by the party as a telling vindication for the years he had already served. Moreover, it would block Blaine, whom Arthur had grown to detest as the chief embodiment of the sentiment against him in the party.

Blaine returned the compliment. His candidacy was in part motivated by a desire to prevent the nomination of Arthur, who, he believed, had dashed Half-Breed hopes for a dynamic administration. Blaine later wrote that the only time he truly wanted the nomination was in 1876, when he had narrowly missed it. Like Arthur, he was haunted by health problems (largely imaginary at this point in his life, but he died of Bright's disease in 1893, six and a half years after Arthur). Blaine also knew that his nomination would rouse the ire of so-called reformers within the Republican Party who would rehash the allegations of corruption leveled against him in 1876. He had scant desire to subject himself to a campaign of vilification. Evidence suggests that what he really preferred was to return to running the State Department, which he had genuinely enjoyed during his ten-month stint in 1881. In the fall of 1883 he had approached at least one potential presidential candidate, and perhaps others, with the offer of support for the nomination in return for appointment as secretary of state. These overtures got nowhere, however, and in early 1884 Blaine entered the race.

With the two leading candidates determined to knock each other off, other men besides Sherman emerged as possible alternatives. Some Stalwarts unwilling to rally to Arthur favored Illinois senator John A. Logan, a former Union general and friend of veterans. Reformers—or "independents"—in the party leaned toward Vermont senator George F. Edmunds, crotchety but principled and best known as a formidable constitutional lawyer in the deliberations of the Judiciary Committee and the Senate at large. Indiana offered two potential favorite sons: Senator Benjamin Harrison, who hoped to inherit Blaine's strength in the event of a deadlock, and Postmaster General Walter Q. Gresham, who hoped to inherit Arthur's.

As the spring wore on, meetings of conventions in the states showed an evident drift toward Blaine. Out of office since December 1881, Blaine had taken no official part in the deliberations over the Mongrel Tariff and thus escaped the embarrassments and criticisms that weighed down the candidacies of his principal rivals, Arthur and Sherman. Yet, in his early fifties, he was not quite ready for elder-statesman status. He had continued to draw attention and exert influence over the Republican Party's outlook in well-chosen speeches, including the formal memorial address for Garfield before a joint session of Congress in 1882. He had spent most of his time as a private citizen writing a book he titled *Twenty Years of Congress*. More a detailed history than a memoir, the two-volume, 1,300-page work focused on the period from 1860 to 1880, but it also included a review of the nation's political history from the framing of the Constitution onward. Appearing in April 1884, two months before the Republican National Convention, the first volume contained a long chapter on the tariff question, in which Blaine sought to solidify his reputation as the party's chief protectionist spokesman—an image he had cultivated since the campaign of 1880. Beginning with the first tariff act passed in 1789, he traced the impact of customs legislation over the succeeding decades. He argued that when protective laws were in force, the country enjoyed prosperity, and when Congress lowered duties, hard times invariably, if sometimes belatedly, ensued. The analysis was simplistic, partaking of politics as much as economics, but Blaine had a point to make: "As a whole, the record of tariff legislation, from the very origin of the government, is the record of enlightened selfishness; and enlightened selfishness is the basis of much that is wisest in legislation."[17]

In the weeks before the 1884 Republican National Convention, rumors arose of a movement to draft General William T. Sherman as the party's presidential nominee. Both Blaine and the general's brother John urged him to accept in the event a call should come, but the general adamantly refused to be considered, and the matter died. When Republican delegates and others poured into Chicago in the first week of June, reporters' straw polls soon showed Blaine clearly in the lead in the delegate count, as he increasingly appeared to be the favorite of the party's masses. He had captured the support of even some Stalwarts estranged from Arthur. Former New York senator Thomas C. Platt had told the president's emissaries asking for support that the party should now let Blaine have his turn.

The platform adopted by the convention laid greatest stress on the tariff issue, in perfect harmony with the sort of campaign Blaine would wage should he receive the nomination. The chairman of the platform committee was a rising star in the party, a Blaine delegate from Ohio named William McKinley, whose labors in Congress on tariff legislation had earned him the sobriquet "Napoleon of Protection." The document demanded that customs duties should be "so levied as to afford security to our diversified industries and protection to the rights and wages of the laborer." The Democrats' program of a tariff "for revenue only," it insisted, "would degrade our labor to the foreign standard." The "importance of sheep husbandry" received special mention, and the platform promised "a readjustment of duties upon foreign wool, in order that such industry shall have full and adequate protection." The Republicans also favored the use of gold and silver as coin at an internationally agreed upon ratio, regulation of railroads, the eight-hour day for labor, aid to education, veterans' pensions, and further extension of civil service reform. The party opposed polygamy and the immigration of contract or Chinese laborers. The platform committee relegated the southern question to the end of the document and called for "such legislation as will secure to every citizen, of whatever race and color, the full and complete recognition, possession and exercise of all civil and political rights."[18]

When at last the delegates turned to selecting a presidential nominee, Blaine led Arthur on the first ballot by 56 votes, but he was still more than 75 votes away from a majority. Edmunds had 93 votes, and Sherman was far behind with 30. The president's only hope was to attract enough support from independents to block Blaine, but his managers in Chicago proved incapable of bringing about a coalition with men who refused to hold their noses and rally to the old spoilsman Arthur. Blaine gained steadily on the next two ballots, after which John A. Logan's withdrawal accelerated the movement, and Blaine was nominated on the fourth ballot. In later proceedings the convention chose Logan for vice president.

More than two hundred delegates stood by Arthur to the end. Although an Arthur delegate had moved that Blaine's nomination be made unanimous, many of the president's supporters left the convention with scant interest in working for the party's ticket. Even

James G. Blaine, the Republican nominee for president in 1884 (Library of Congress)

more embittered were the independents who had convinced themselves of the truth of allegations of corruption in the nominee's record as a public man. As Blaine's victory was announced, Carl
Schurz, sitting on the platform, consulted his watch and declared,
"From this hour dates the death of the Republican party."[19] But
Schurz was in the minority among Republicans. Blaine's fervent
supporters, known as Blainiacs, were convinced that he had the
charisma and the energy and the issue in the tariff to carry the party
to victory.

In the equilibrium that marked the nation's politics, Blaine's
chances would, of course, depend in great measure on the nominations made by the Democrats. To some degree, the preconvention
campaign that took shape within the Democratic Party in the spring
of 1884 looked like a reprise of the Democratic contest of 1880.
Samuel J. Tilden still enjoyed enormous affection among the party
faithful, but he was now past seventy years old, and his health had
grown even less robust in the last four years. Most of the speculation
that swirled around Tilden concerned who would inherit his supporters. As in 1880, the lineup included the stolid Thomas F. Bayard, the protectionist Samuel J. Randall, and Tilden's old running
mate, Thomas A. Hendricks, but again none of these men sparked
much enthusiasm. Neither did such state favorite sons as former senator Joseph E. McDonald of Indiana, House Speaker John G. Carlisle
of Kentucky, or former Ohio senator Allen G. Thurman, who, though
popular, was older than Tilden and equally unlikely to revitalize the
party for victory.

Handicappers of the race also gave attention to a new potential
contender, Governor Grover Cleveland of New York, although in the
early speculation he was mentioned as much for the vice presidency
as for the presidency. Cleveland's rise to prominence had been recent
and rapid. A lawyer from Buffalo, he had served as county sheriff in
the early 1870s. He lacked flair and flash, but he gained a reputation for honesty, hard work, and commitment to the Democratic
Party. In 1881, when an anti-machine group convinced him to run

for mayor of Buffalo, he ran and won on the reform issue. In office, he vetoed extravagant appropriations and otherwise burnished his image as an exemplar of good government. That image served him well the next year, when state Democrats chose him as an indisputably clean candidate for governor to run against Charles J. Folger, the Republican handpicked by the Arthur administration. Touching only lightly on state issues, Cleveland emphasized civil service reform in his campaign. Inevitably, his landslide victory tended to nourish his and others' inflated sense that he was a different sort of leader, a tribune of the people rather than a mere politician. As governor, Cleveland further cultivated this image, frequently using his veto to block what he considered reckless or flawed legislation. In addition, he engaged in a bitter fight over patronage with Tammany Hall, the very citadel of political depravity in the eyes of good citizens, not only in New York but throughout the country. As Blaine emerged as the likely nominee of the Republicans in 1884, increasing numbers of Democrats bought into the idea that "Grover the Good" might be just the man to take on "the Continental Liar from the State of Maine."

Tilden finally issued a formal declination of the nomination in early June, and many regarded Cleveland as the logical legatee to his support. By the time the national convention met a month later, the governor had achieved substantial momentum. At the gathering in Chicago, the most clamorous opposition came from the Tammany delegates, a circumstance that played directly into the hands of Cleveland's managers. One of the speakers for Cleveland proudly declared that the rising young men of the party "love him most for the enemies that he has made."[20] Cleveland had a substantial lead on the first ballot and easily took the nomination on the second. For vice president, the delegates chose Hendricks, the 1876 nominee.

In preparing the party's platform, the resolutions committee recognized the potency of the Republicans' protectionist arguments and abandoned the Democrats' simplistic "tariff for revenue only" formula of 1880. Hoping to please all sections of the party, the committee said that taxation should "be limited to the requirements of economical government" but that in making reductions, "it is not proposed to injure any domestic industries" or to deprive "American labor of the ability to compete successfully with foreign labor." With an eye to the Irish American vote, the platform writers condemned protectionism as "the Republican party's British policy," in that it curtailed the ability of American producers to compete with British counterparts in world markets. Nonetheless, many of the Democrats' true believers in tariff reduction regarded the tariff plank as a meaningless straddle. In other provisions, the platform favored a currency consisting of gold and silver coin and paper convertible into coin, "honest Civil Service Reform," and federal improvements of the Mississippi and other waterways. It denounced land grants to railroads, sumptuary laws, and the importation of foreign labor, especially "Mongolians."[21]

As in previous elections, the two major parties were forced to weigh the impact of third-party tickets. The Greenback Labor Party nominated former Massachusetts congressman and governor Benjamin Butler, who had by turns been a Republican and a Democrat. Somewhat erratic, but known to sympathize with the downtrodden, Butler had harbored a faint hope for the Democratic nomination. Many Republicans were not sorry to see him in the field, where they believed he could draw votes from Cleveland. For their part, Democrats hoped that Prohibition Party candidate John P. St. John would siphon anti-liquor cold-water voters away from Blaine. Given the even balance between the Republicans and the Democrats, such potential defections, especially in the doubtful states, haunted the calculations of the major party managers.

Republican reckoning was further disturbed by the attitude of the party's independent wing. Shortly after Cleveland's nomination, a portion of the independents and other reform representatives gathered in New York to plot their strategy for the coming campaign. The group issued a statement declaring that Blaine was "an unfit leader . . . who has traded upon his official trust for his pecuniary gain; a representative of men, methods, and conduct which the public conscience condemns." Cleveland, by contrast, was "one whose name is the synonym of political courage and honesty and of administrative reform." With this meeting, the Mugwumps, so named from an Indian word for "leader," launched a campaign that they relentlessly pursued to prevent Blaine from ever reaching the White House. Foremost in the effort was Carl Schurz, who gave speech after speech, even bringing to light new "Mulligan Letters" to illustrate Blaine's supposed corrupt dealings. Democrats were ecstatic. Their candidate was a relative newcomer, had never held federal office, and was not closely associated with any national issue such as the tariff or the currency. As he had done in his previous bids for office, Cleveland intended to make the character issue the centerpiece of his campaign. Thus he and the Democrats could take special joy from the New York conference's solemn avowal that "the paramount issue of the Presidential election of this year is moral rather than political."[22]

Immediately, however, the Mugwump project suffered an enormous jolt. As the delegates left the New York conference, they were handed copies of a Buffalo newspaper with a sensational story under the headline A TERRIBLE TALE, which alleged that ten years earlier Cleveland had sired an illegitimate child with one Maria Halpin, a widowed mother of two children.[23] Cleveland never denied the allegation, and its truth was generally accepted. His defenders, including the Mugwumps, insisted that the incident, though damnable, was an aberration rather than part of a pattern. (Indeed, Cleveland's determination in the mid-1870s to rebound from the potential political and social consequences of the lapse may well have impelled him to adopt his almost obsessive commitment to uprightness and duty.) After some soul-searching, most Mugwumps and Democrats convinced themselves that Blaine's supposed violation of a public

Another voice for Cleveland.

The Republican magazine *Judge* lampoons "Grover the Good" for the moral lapse in his private life. (*Judge*, September 27, 1884)

trust was a far graver and more disqualifying offense than Cleveland's private turpitude. Dipping down into the mud themselves, some Democrats spread the tale that Mrs. Blaine had given birth to the couple's first child only three months after their marriage. The campaign quickly degenerated into one of the dirtiest in American history.

The candidates themselves strove to remain above the smears. Never at ease on the stump, Cleveland made few speeches and avoided saying much about issues. In his formal letter of acceptance he avoided the tariff question and gave only faint echoes of the platform on other issues such as civil service and Chinese immigration. In one speech toward the end of the campaign he declared that "necessary reduction in taxation . . . should be effected without depriving American labor of the ability to compete successfully with foreign labor." But on the eve of the election he returned to the character issue, labeling his Republican opponents as "a vast army of office-holders, long in power" and "corrupt to the core."[24]

Although Blaine was a much more seasoned candidate, his campaign confronted serious obstacles. Besides the Mugwump desertion, the Arthur administration showed little disposition to lend its aid, and a slowdown in the economy led voters to blame the Republicans as the party in power. Blaine strove mightily to surmount these hurdles and to elevate the tone of the campaign, primarily by focusing on economic issues. He devoted more than half of his letter of acceptance to the tariff question alone. He made "protection to American labor" the "one great issue" of the campaign in the state elections in his home state of Maine, where in September the voters "responded nobly," giving the Republicans a smashing victory. For the next two months Blaine took the unusual step of conducting a campaign speaking tour, carrying his tariff message as far west as Wisconsin. Initially he said relatively little about the southern question. Perceiving that personal animus against him might cost him critical doubtful states such as New York, Blaine forbore waving the

bloody shirt in hopes of compensating for northern losses by crack-
ing the Solid South. He urged southerners, especially in the Border
States and Upper South, to bury past sectional animosities and recognize the benefits of Republican protectionism for their rising ex-
tractive and manufacturing industries. He particularly targeted the
iron fields and coalfields of West Virginia, where he asked voters
which they would prefer, "to gratify a prejudice or to promote general prosperity?" Enough apparently preferred the former, for the
state election in October resulted in a victory for the Democratic
ticket by four percentage points.[25]

Undaunted, Blaine continued his tour, still emphasizing the tariff issue but also sprinkling his speeches in the Midwest with refer-
ences to the sectional question. He warned northerners not to entrust
the nation's economic interests "to the old South, with its bitterness,
its unreconciled temper," and "its absolute incapacity to measure
the sweep and the magnitude of our great future."[26] The tour was a
great success, drawing large, enthusiastic crowds. At its end in New
York, however, disaster struck.

Blaine, like other Republicans, had tried to win the support of
British-hating Irish American Democrats by insisting that the
Democrats' call for a reduced tariff was essentially equivalent to
the British advocacy of free trade. At the Fifth Avenue Hotel on the
morning of October 29, a week before the election, in a staged event
designed to take the edge off the character issue, Blaine appeared
publicly to receive the endorsement of a large gathering of Protestant ministers. Unfortunately, the group's spokesman declared, "We
are Republicans, and don't propose to leave our party and identify
ourselves with the party whose antecedents have been Rum, Roman-
ism, and Rebellion." Blaine failed to catch and immediately rebuke
this slur against Roman Catholicism, the faith of most Irish Americans. Democratic reporters on the scene made sure the incident was
splashed in the newspapers the next day. Blaine eventually repudi-
ated the insult, noting that his own mother had been a Catholic, but

it was hard to undo the damage. Later on the same day, Blaine attended a lavish dinner at New York's Delmonico's restaurant, where he hoped (in vain, as it turned out) to raise campaign funds from some of the nation's wealthiest capitalists, who, he frankly told them, had made "marvelous progress" thanks to Republican tariff policies. Democrats had a field day, insisting that the event gave the lie to Blaine's claim that protectionism primarily benefited labor. The next day the *New York World* carried a front-page cartoon depicting "The Royal Feast of Belshazzar Blaine and the Money Kings," with a poor family begging for scraps in front of a groaning banquet table.[27]

The impact of these last-minute episodes is impossible to gauge with precision, but over the course of the campaign Blaine had done much to overcome the obstacles he confronted. On election day he lost to Cleveland by one of the narrowest margins in history. The electoral college gave 219 votes to Cleveland and 182 to Blaine, with New York's 36 electors providing the winning margin. Cleveland had carried that state's popular vote by only 1,047 out of more than 1 million votes cast. The outcome was so close that any number of factors could have tipped the balance. Following the established pattern, the nationwide result was largely sectional. Cleveland won all the former slave states plus the doubtful states of New York, Indiana, Connecticut, and New Jersey. Blaine won all the other states in the North and the West. In a postelection speech, Blaine blamed the result on the political repression in the South, which "has crushed out the political power of more than 6,000,000 American citizens, and has transferred it by violence to others."[28] Yet a close examination of the returns suggested that Blaine's original southern strategy was not necessarily foolhardy. The percentage of the vote he received in the three southern states of Tennessee, Virginia, and West Virginia taken together was actually greater than the percentage he received in the four northern doubtful states taken together. He lost Tennessee by under 4 percentage points and Virginia by just

2.2 points. Had he won both of them, he could have taken the presidency without any of the northern doubtful states.

If either candidate had coattails in the congressional elections, it was Blaine. The Democrats retained control of the House but saw their numbers decline by more than fifteen, while the Republicans gained more than twenty. Little change occurred in the southern delegations; the Republicans gained seats in the North, where Blaine had concentrated his campaign. Republicans increased their majority in the Senate to eight seats more than the Democrats.

With Cleveland's victory so narrow, no group within or outside his party could claim preponderant credit for putting him over the top. Thus the president-elect could not unnaturally picture himself as his own man, indebted to no particular individual or interest for his victory. Over the years, the self-righteous Cleveland had fashioned a political persona as a lonely and principled tribune of the people, seemingly always at bay against nefarious forces that threatened his notions of the public good. As he prepared to enter the White House, he wrote to a friend, "I look upon the four years next to come as a dreadful self-inflicted penance for the good of my country. I can see no pleasure in it and no satisfaction, only a hope that I may be of service to my people."[29]

FOUR

Grover Cleveland: The Last Jacksonian

Few presidents have entered upon their duties with less experience in national affairs than Grover Cleveland. He had never served in the cabinet or in Congress or, indeed, in any federal office. His brief public career had been limited to state and local government, primarily in executive positions. He had never served in a legisla ture and had never really learned the give-and-take of the legis- lative process. During his campaign for the White House he had pushed himself as a certain kind of leader—honest, selfless, and dedicated—rather than as an advocate of a particular agenda. He entered the presidency with a much less developed sense of pro- gram and policy than that of his defeated opponent, James G. Blaine. After a conversation with the president-elect, a Mugwump newspa- per editor concluded that on "the great mass of National questions, which will come up for daily treatment, his information is extremely defective."[1]

All this is not to say that Cleveland had no principles, for he adhered to the time-honored tenets of the Democratic Party. Govern- ment, he believed, should be small and frugal and focused at the state and local level. He subscribed to the classic liberal notion of natural and enduring economic laws, with which government should not interfere. Although he had said little about economic issues in his campaign, he tended to view Republican policies such as the protective tariff and subsidies as abuses of power on behalf of favored interests to the detriment of others. In short, Cleveland espoused a public philosophy not much different from that proclaimed by the Jacksonian Democrats fifty years earlier. Nor was Cleveland's conception of the presidency much different from that of Andrew Jackson himself. Like Jackson, Cleveland saw himself as the only official elected by all the people, one whose principal function was to defend them from corrupt interests. Like the Old Hero, he viewed the national executive as the chief safeguard against congressional excess. During his first term he vetoed more than four hundred bills, more than twice the number vetoed by all his predecessors combined.

One of the most trying jobs confronting a new president was making appointments to the thousands of federal offices, and as the first Democrat elected to the presidency since James Buchanan in 1856, Cleveland found the task particularly troublesome. Democratic Party workers, shut out of federal patronage for more than a generation, eagerly anticipated at last enjoying the spoils of office. Yet during the campaign Cleveland had cultivated the support of civil service reformers, many of whom were Mugwumps who had abandoned the Republicans to support the Democratic nominee. Believing that Cleveland owed his election to them, the reformers urged him to expand the merit system. They particularly hoped that he would not fire Republican officeholders wholesale simply to make way for Democrats.

The new president initially tilted toward the reformers' ideas, promising to enforce the Pendleton Act and to leave Republicans in place until the end of their terms, with one key proviso—that they abstain from engaging in "offensive partisanship." Cleveland did not initiate a mass turnover in the offices early in his term, and reformers were generally pleased. But Democratic Party bosses and workers grew increasingly insistent in demanding patronage recognition, and before long the administration began to dismiss Republicans in large numbers, in many cases invoking the "offensive partisanship" standard. Outraged Republicans in Congress demanded evidence of wrongdoing by the fired employees, which Cleveland adamantly refused to provide. In one notorious incident, the administration ousted a poor Union army veteran's widow from her job as postmistress in a small town in Indiana. In Congress, Senator Benjamin Harrison delivered an impassioned rebuke to Cleveland for the heartless dismissal, declaring that "there is not a Democratic Senator here who would not scorn to be the author of such treatment."[2]

Although Cleveland's refusal to divulge his reasons for political dismissals struck a blow for executive independence, Republicans naturally accused him of hypocrisy in his reform pretensions, and many reformers felt betrayed. Mugwumps such as Carl Schurz began to fear that "this 'reform Administration' will end like its predecessors: sit down between two chairs — do just enough to disgust the enemies of reform and not enough to satisfy its friends." But once Cleveland had begun to give offices to Democrats, he found that he could satisfy only a fraction of the applicants, and many who went away empty-handed also felt betrayed. "It's mighty hard to get along with the Democrats of a locality," he complained, "when different factions are tattling and finding fault with each other like a mess of schoolboys." In the end, Cleveland's handling of the patronage did little to build a large personal following that would enhance his prospects for reelection in 1888.[3]

Neither did the money question inure to Cleveland's political benefit. In 1878 the Bland-Allison Act had mandated the limited but steady coinage of silver dollars. After a half decade of such coinage, hard-money forces had begun to fear that the government's acceptance of silver in payment of taxes, coupled with its commitment to pay its main obligations in gold, could deplete the Treasury's gold supply for greenback redemption and undermine the gold standard. The solution, they believed, was to suspend silver coinage. Such a proposal, put before Congress on the eve of Cleveland's inauguration, alarmed soft-money interests, and a group of ninety-five pro-silver Democratic congressmen urged the president-elect to come out against it. Instead, Cleveland endorsed the proposed suspension, arguing that continued coinage could lead to "prolonged and disastrous trouble."[4] His public letter aroused the ire of House Democrats, who voted two to one against suspension. As president, Cleveland continued to call for an end to coinage, but he failed to unite his party on the issue. Indeed, in the spring of 1886, when the House considered a bill not to suspend, but to institute free coinage of silver, Democrats favored it by a vote of 98 to 70. Although an upswing in the nation's economy undermined the inflationists' appeal, Democrats remained deeply divided on the silver question.

In some respects, Cleveland's accession to the presidency represented a step in the neutralization of the southern question. In its most virulent form, Republican bloody shirt rhetoric had warned that the Democrats' coming into power would revive the spirit of the southern rebellion. Initially Cleveland sought to allay such anxieties. Twenty years after Appomattox, he expressed the hope in his inaugural address that "from this hour we cheerfully and honestly abandon all sectional prejudice and distrust." For his cabinet he selected three southerners—two of whom had held office in the Confederacy—not as a mark of approbation of the rebellion, but as a manifestation of reconciliation between the North and South. It was time, he said, to "work out harmoniously the achievements of our national destiny."[5]

And yet Cleveland never forgot that the great preponderance of his party's strength and of his own support for reelection lay in the South. Fully aware of the effectiveness of Blaine's economic southern strategy in 1884, Cleveland took care in trying to maintain the Democrats' southern base. Although he declared in his inaugural that "there should be no pretext for anxiety touching the protection of the freedmen in their rights," the Justice Department, led by an attorney general who had served four years in the Confederate Congress, did comparatively little to uphold voting rights laws in the region.[6]

Even more offensive to many northerners was Cleveland's approach to the question of government pensions for disabled Union military veterans. Since the war, the federal Pension Bureau had issued pensions to hundreds of thousands of injured veterans who could not support themselves. On occasions when the bureau rejected an individual's application, he could try to get a special bill for a pension passed by Congress. Cleveland, unlike his Republican predecessors, vetoed hundreds of these pension bills, sometimes in mocking language, on the grounds that the individual cases did not meet the disability stipulations of the pension rules. In early 1887 Congress passed legislation to clarify those rules and broaden their application, but Cleveland vetoed that bill as well. "The race after the pensions offered by this bill," he declared, "would not only stimulate weakness and pretended incapacity for labor, but put a further premium on dishonesty and mendacity."[7] Mugwump supporters of government frugality hailed the veto, as did southerners who bristled at paying taxes to cover benefits closed to themselves. But the action naturally incurred the wrath of veterans throughout the North. Even within Cleveland's own party, many northerners saw the president's policy as wrongheaded and politically disastrous, and more than fifty Democrats voted for the dependent pension bill. (Cleveland's punctiliousness regarding the public purse was not limited to pensions. Two weeks later he vetoed a bill appropriating $10,000 to provide seeds to aid drought-stricken farmers. "Though the people support the Government," he declared, "the Government should not support the people.")[8]

Union veterans organizations, which were among the largest and most potent interest groups, took the lead in denouncing Cleveland's pension vetoes. Four months after the dependent bill veto, the president fueled their ire even more when he signed off on an order to send captured Confederate battle flags stored in the War Department back to the southern states. However much Cleveland may have intended this move as a gesture of sectional reconciliation, Union veterans saw it as a callous act that lent sanctity to the treasonous cause they had struggled, and their comrades had died, to suppress. The leader of the Grand Army of the Republic, the largest veterans group, declared, "May God palsy the hand that wrote that order. May God palsy the brain that conceived it, and may God palsy the tongue that dictated it." Many Republican politicians joined the chorus of condemnation, not merely in reaction to the flag order but also out of their continuing resentment over Cleveland's 1884 victory based in large part on the South, which they believed "was made 'solid' by bloody and fraudulent methods." Outside the South, even some Democrats expressed their dismay that, as one Colorado group put it, Cleveland was "only seen as a representative of rebellion, a viper, and an untrustworthy man."[9]

Later in 1887 the president once again moved to invigorate his southern base. To fill a Supreme Court vacancy, he chose Mississippi Confederate veteran L.Q.C. Lamar, who had been serving in his cabinet as secretary of the Interior. Lamar had enjoyed a reputation as a southern moderate in Congress after the war, but he nonetheless espoused southern Democratic doctrine regarding voting rights and related issues. His relatively advanced age, sixty-two, uncertain health, and marginal legal expertise all indicated that Cleveland turned to him primarily for his appeal below the Mason-Dixon Line. Southerners were pleased, but Republicans denounced an appointment that they thought sullied the judicial ermine. "No man," one Republican senator insisted, "ought to be confirmed to the Supreme Court whose *status* as to the validity of the Constitutional amendments growing out of the war is open to question."[10] But Cleveland stuck by Lamar, who narrowly won confirmation in the Senate with the help of two defecting Republicans and a Virginia independent.

Cleveland may have approached running for a second term in 1888 with his southern base intact, but as in 1884, he would need to find support outside the region in order to win. This need seemed even clearer after the 1886 midterm congressional elections, in which the Democrats lost fifteen seats in the House. Although the party's hold on the South remained steady, one-third of its losses occurred in the key doubtful states of New York and Indiana. One issue that might have helped Cleveland was the growing demand for federal regulation of the railroads. Many Americans who had come to depend on these railroads were increasingly angered by the companies' unfair and ravenous practices. Congress debated methods of regulation for years, and President Arthur had pushed for legislation to curtail the roads' "unjust and oppressive" methods. Cleveland, however, failed to take the lead on the question, merely telling Congress that the subject was "worthy of consideration."[11] In January 1887, lopsided bipartisan majorities in both houses passed the Interstate Commerce Act, establishing the federal government's first regulatory commission. Without fanfare, Cleveland affixed his signature. He could take little credit for the law and thus chose not to make railroad regulation an element in his campaign for reelection. He knew that deep party divisions precluded emphasis on the money question in the coming campaign, while antagonism between Mugwumps and party regulars ruled out the issue of civil service reform. As the presidential election year approached, it was clear that the president needed to find some winning issue, and he finally hit upon tariff reduction as the most likely rallying point to unite his party and reformers against the Republicans.

As a newcomer to national affairs, Cleveland had entered the White House with only a passing familiarity with the tariff issue. Before taking office, he confessed his ignorance to Carl Schurz, who provided him with a list of books on the subject. Cleveland was a diligent student, but he did not launch a tariff "reform" crusade immediately. His first annual message echoed the straddle of the 1884

THE OPENING OF THE CONGRESSIONAL SESSION.
Tariff Monster.—Here I am again!! What are you going to do with me?

The Democratic magazine *Puck* depicts the monstrous surplus plaguing the nation at the opening of Congress in December 1887. (*Puck*, December 7, 1887)

Democratic platform: a call to reduce customs duties but in ways not destructive to American industry and labor. In the spring of 1886 Cleveland backed a bill in the House calling for substantial tariff reductions, but it lost by a vote of 140 to 157, with 35 Democrats, led by Pennsylvania congressman Samuel J. Randall, joining the Republicans to kill the measure. The existence of a vocal minority of protectionists among Democrats in Congress and in the nation complicated Cleveland's approach to the tariff both as a matter of public policy and as a campaign issue.

The pressing predicament behind the drive for reduction was the continuing large surplus in the federal budget, which for fiscal 1888 was projected to be $100 million, or 30 percent of total receipts. Such excessive revenues, Cleveland said, threatened to leave "a vast quantity" of the people's money "hoarded in the Treasury when it should be in their hands." A severe stringency in the nation's money markets in the summer of 1887 threatened to ignite a general panic and convinced Cleveland of the critical condition of the government's finances. Temporary Treasury Department operations alleviated the immediate crisis, but the president was determined to demand a long-term solution through substantial revenue reduction when Congress came back into session. In the interim, state elections offered a test of the political viability of a movement for tariff reform. In both New York and Ohio, Democrats called for large cuts in the tariff and placed the issue prominently in their campaigns. The New York State ticket won a commanding victory, but in Ohio the Democrats lost by a wider margin. The defeated candidate for governor in Ohio urged the president to "go slow" on the question of tariff revision to avoid "the danger of alienating large bodies of workmen," but Cleveland decided to take his cue from his home state.[12]

In early December 1887 Cleveland sent Congress his third annual message, devoted entirely to the single subject of the tariff. He began with a discussion of the perils of the huge Treasury surplus and declared that whittling it down through increased expenditures would amount to "reckless improvidence." He also rejected reducing internal taxation on alcohol and tobacco. Instead, he insisted that "our present tariff laws, the vicious, inequitable, and illogical source of unnecessary taxation, ought to be at once revised and amended." Current high rates, he implied, permitted manufacturing interests, "without regard to the public welfare," to realize "immense profits instead of moderately profitable returns." Lower duties would result in lower prices for consumers and allow manufacturers to purchase cheaper raw materials, which would in turn enable them to reduce the prices they charged and thus compete more effectively in world markets. Denying that high duties prevented wages of Americans from falling to the level of "what is called the pauper labor of Europe," he claimed that only 15 percent of the nation's labor force worked in industries affected by the tariff, and that even these were "consumers with the rest." The country required a tariff that would restore to the economy the excess money collected and piled up in the Treasury. Fully cognizant of the debate his proposal would spark, Cleveland admonished his countrymen to avoid "bandying epithets" or "dwelling upon the theories of protection and free trade." "It is," he declared, "a *condition* which confronts us, not a theory."[13]

Republicans, however, were hardly content to allow the president to set the limits of the debate. James G. Blaine immediately labeled the message "a free trade manifesto" that portended "an enlarged market" for British goods. Traveling in Europe, Blaine held a newspaper interview in which he answered Cleveland's message point by point. He called for the immediate repeal of the tobacco tax, which would offer great relief to southern growers as well as laboring men across the country who considered tobacco a necessity. He would not repeal the levies on alcohol, however, invoking the "moral side" of the question to appeal to temperance advocates. Surplus revenues, Blaine said, could underwrite needed improvements in coastal fortifications, which would improve the country's defense and also provide work for labor. He warned that if Congress were to implement Cleveland's recommendations, the country would suffer a "deluging inflow" of foreign goods that would bring "the destruction of home industry" and "drive our own workmen from mechanical and manufacturing pursuits." Laborers would be forced to "become tillers of the soil," and farmers would thus suffer from a "glutting" of their markets. Reprising a theme from his 1884 campaign, Blaine urged southerners "to sit down and calculate the value of Democratic free trade to their local interests." The region had vast potential for developing industry, but, he warned, "they cannot do anything without protection." Overall, Blaine insisted, the president's pronouncement made clear that "the Democratic party in power is a standing menace to the industrial prosperity of the country." In their 1884 campaign Cleveland had largely avoided the tariff issue that Blaine had emphasized; now, said Blaine, he had made it "the one issue" for the presidential campaign about to begin.[14]

In general, Cleveland's message delighted Republicans, who were eager to fight their opponents in a battle that directly pitted protection against "free trade." Indeed, the message unified Republicans more than Democrats. The majority of the president's party responded favorably to his call to arms, but a substantial minority did not. "Our fat friend at the White House has settled his own hash for 1888," a Pennsylvania Democrat complained to Congressman Randall. "I hope he will be nominated so that no worthy Democrat may have to take the defeat he so well deserves and has rendered inevitable." The protectionist Randall refused to toe the line and promised to introduce revenue-reduction legislation that would cut import duties somewhat, but, he said, a "large part of this reduction will be in the repeal of internal taxes which the President does not seem to favor." In less than two weeks, Cleveland was "fearful almost to conviction that our people in Congress will so botch and blunder upon the tariff question that all the benefit of the stand already taken will not be realized." He ordered Secretary of State

Thomas Bayard to press treaty negotiations to halt illegal immigration of workers from China. If his tariff initiative failed, Cleveland hoped that "a proper movement upon the Chinese question would furnish a compensation in the way of another string to our bow."[15]

Cleveland's bid for a renomination met with some grumbling from opponents within his party. Protectionist Democrats found more to like in Samuel Randall than in Grover Cleveland, and machine-oriented men who bridled at the president's civil service tendencies warmed to the unabashed partisanship of New York governor David B. Hill. Neither of these incipient challenges had a realistic chance of defeating the president, but Cleveland's men nonetheless came down hard on both. In Pennsylvania they elbowed Randall's allies out of leadership positions in the state party; in New York they did the same and even denied Hill a seat on the state's delegation at the national convention. Such actions were hardly calculated to secure the enthusiastic support of these groups in the later general election campaign.

Protectionist opposition in part reflected dismay with the course of tariff legislation in Congress in the wake of Cleveland's message. In the early spring, Texas congressman Roger Mills, chairman of the House Ways and Means Committee, introduced a bill that would cut internal levies by $24 million and reduce tariff revenue by $54 million, either by reducing rates or putting imported items on the duty-free list. Mills and five other southern Democrats on the committee gave the new rates in the bill a decidedly southern tinge. It made only minor reductions for imports that competed with commodities that southerners produced, such as sugar, iron ore, coal, tobacco, and rice, while calling for large cuts on items southerners purchased, such as hemp bagging and metal ties used in baling cotton. The bill also slashed duties on items produced in the Midwest, such as lumber, salt, hemp, flax, and, most important, wool. Through the summer and into the fall, the Mills bill dominated congressional debate, which provided a backdrop for the ongoing political campaign.

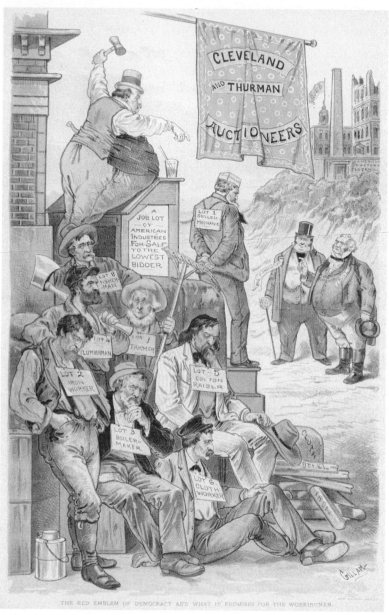

Judge depicts the auctioneer Grover Cleveland selling out American industries and workers for the benefit of bloated English manufacturers. (*Judge*, July 14, 1888)

Although the majority of Democrats in Congress rallied around the Mills bill and Cleveland's tariff policy, party campaigners in some areas found the program to be a hard sell. An early important test came in the state elections in April 1888 in Rhode Island, a state with large manufacturing interests. After running a campaign in line with Cleveland's message, the incumbent Democratic governor lost his bid for reelection by eight percentage points. He reported to Cleveland that "able orators were imported into the State and 'revenue reform' as advocated by us was denounced as 'free trade' which mill operatives and others have been learned to look upon as predetermined ruin to them."[16] Other northern Democrats heeded the lesson. In three important doubtful states, Indiana, New Jersey, and Connecticut, Democratic state conventions issued platforms that omitted mention of the Mills bill, and in the latter two states they also dodged mention of Cleveland's message. Instead, they endorsed the 1884 national platform plank on the issue, which called for revenue reduction but gave much more space to reassurance that reform should be cautious so as to preserve American industry and labor.

By mid-May, with the national convention just a few weeks away, Cleveland conceded the need to moderate the party's stand. For the New York Democratic state convention, he dictated a platform that endorsed his message but also cited the 1884 national platform and made no mention of the word *tariff* or the Mills bill, which had become a lightning rod for protectionist attack.

Cleveland had less luck controlling the national convention. On the eve of that gathering in St. Louis, the need for moderation seemed even more acute when Oregon Democrats, who had waged a state campaign focused distinctly on the tariff and Cleveland's message, went down to resounding defeat. Again Cleveland drafted a platform and commissioned a leading protectionist Democrat, Arthur Gorman, and a moderate reductionist, William Scott, to push his views before the platform committee in St. Louis. Cleveland's opening paragraph on the tariff ignored his message and the Mills bill and simply reaffirmed the party's 1884 platform. But this evasion was unacceptable to the low-tariff forces on the committee who threatened a floor fight if the text was not changed. After hours of wrangling, the two sides arrived at a text that retained the endorsement of the 1884 platform but cited Cleveland's message as the "correct interpretation of that platform" and also endorsed the efforts of congressional Democrats to "secure a reduction of excessive taxation." The low-tariff men were satisfied, but the spectacle of the president's representatives fighting against a specific endorsement of his own policy statement sent voters a confused signal. As *The New York Times* put it, "This little game is not easy to understand."[17]

Other planks in Cleveland's draft stirred controversy as well. On the question of civil service, Cleveland said that appointments should recognize "fidelity and efficiency . . . instead of the claims of partisanship." In its final form, the platform merely commended the president for elevating "the public service to the highest standard of efficiency." In a gesture toward national reconciliation, Cleveland's draft referred to the equality of citizens before the law "without regard to race or color." The plank's final version read "without regard to race or section," thereby reflecting persistent white southern resentment over supposed ill-treatment after the Civil War.[18]

No suspense attended Cleveland's renomination. Although some of his policies had not pleased all Democrats, the party was not about to abandon the only man it had placed in the White House since the mid-1850s. His nomination sparked a prolonged and spirited demonstration on the convention floor. In choosing a running mate, the delegates bowed to Cleveland's wishes and nominated former Ohio senator Allen G. Thurman. The reasons for Cleveland's choice are not altogether clear. Thurman was seventy-four years old, and his health was far from robust. Cleveland may have thought that Thurman would give the ticket a boost in Ohio, although over the years Thurman had made enemies in his home state. He was popular in New York, where he might help Cleveland among party regulars, and on the West Coast, where citizens appreciated his support for restriction of Chinese immigration. Having entered politics in the age of Jackson, Thurman enjoyed widespread affection among Democrats as the party's "Old Roman," so despite his infirmities, the delegates enthusiastically endorsed his nomination.

When the race for the Republican nomination began to take shape in late 1887, many people in both parties predicted a rematch between Cleveland and James G. Blaine. Although Cleveland had won his narrow victory by taking New York by the slenderest of margins, myriad Republicans still believed that the suppression of the black vote in the South had allowed the Democrats to steal the presidency in 1884. Many who were determined to right that perceived wrong welcomed Blaine's spirited condemnation of Cleveland's tariff message as a declaration by the Plumed Knight that he was once again ready to clamp on his armor and battle for the party. Yet to nearly everyone's surprise, in January, Blaine, still sojourning in Europe, wrote a letter from Florence to the Republican national chairman stating that his name would "not be presented" to the Republican National Convention. The former nominee did not relish the expense, personal attack, or drain on his health that another national campaign would entail. He "abhor[red] the idea of becoming a chronic candidate," and he told friends that he was not even sure that he wanted to be president. And yet his Florence letter did not say he would refuse if drafted by the convention, and he hinted to a few intimates, such as *New York Tribune* proprietor Whitelaw Reid, that he might accept a nomination if it were unanimous or nearly so, although he considered that unlikely. Conflicting evidence suggests that Blaine was not entirely clear in his own mind what he wanted, and his aggrieved supporters were reluctant to give him up. Throughout the spring of 1888, a loyal group headed by Reid and Stephen B. Elkins, Blaine's 1884 manager, worked behind the scenes and in the press to keep the possibility of a Blaine nomination alive.[19]

Rivals for the Republican nomination, though, were inclined to take Blaine's withdrawal at face value. Even before the Florence letter, John Sherman had entered the field, and at age sixty-five he knew that this would be his last chance. Iowa senator William B. Allison, chairman of the Appropriations Committee, enjoyed renown as a financial expert and an adroit legislative craftsman, but his bland personality sparked little popular enthusiasm beyond his home state. Some eastern party leaders also doubted his commitment to orthodox protectionism. The list of Republican aspirants included at least two men of substantial wealth: former governor Russell Alger of Michigan, who had made millions in lumber and other enterprises, and Chauncey Depew, president of the New York Central Railroad. At a time when citizens' resentment of "monopoly" power was growing, neither Alger nor Depew had a realistic chance to head the party's ticket. More likely to appeal to the disaffected was federal judge Walter Q. Gresham, who had dealt Jay Gould a defeat in court and had won esteem as a friend of labor by defending the rights of strikers. But Gresham's tariff views did not square with the party's high protectionism, and Blaine's friends disliked him, in large part because as a member of Arthur's cabinet, Gresham had done little to help the Plumed Knight in the 1884 campaign.

The preferences of the Blaine contingent, the largest wing in the party, would prove immensely important, especially if Blaine himself were truly out of the running. No one appreciated the significance of the Blaine element more than the supporters of Benjamin Harrison, grandson of President William Henry Harrison. Harrison enjoyed obvious name recognition and hailed from the doubtful state of Indiana, which had taken on added importance after the Republicans lost the 1887 state elections in New York. Harrison had served one term in the Senate, where his ability to expound party doctrine caught the notice of his Republican colleagues. A well-to-do and respected lawyer, he had for years spoken effectively on the stump in his own state and elsewhere. A favorite son possibility in the 1884 convention, he had thrown his support to Blaine at a critical moment and afterward had campaigned hard for the nominee. Thus, Harrison's backers believed that he had a special claim to the Plumed Knight's favor.

And indeed, Blaine had taken notice. In early March, Blaine had sent Elkins his assessment of the field of candidates. Sherman lacked popularity as well as sympathy with Blaine's allies, Gresham harbored an "unjust hostility to corporations," and Allison's tariff record would "destroy the effort of the party to make a campaign for Protection." After dismissing several favorite son candidates, Blaine concluded that "the one man remaining, who in my judgment can make the best run, is Ben Harrison."[20] Blaine did not mention that he harbored hopes for a return to the State Department in a Harrison administration, but the thought had no doubt occurred to him. Even before Elkins received Blaine's letter, he had been in contact with the Harrison campaign, telling the former senator and his managers that many Blaine men thought highly of Harrison as a potential nominee. The Hoosiers welcomed the compliment but were nonetheless wary of Elkins's real intentions.

In the months before the national convention, Elkins continued this flirtation, hoping to bring the two camps together at the convention, ultimately with Blaine at the top of the ticket. Elkins, Reid, and others had arrived at an implicit strategy of working for a deadlocked convention, which would eventually turn to Blaine with a nomination he could not refuse. If the strategy failed, the Blaine men viewed Harrison as a more than acceptable second choice, who would be amenable to the Blaine wing of the party. In late May, Blaine issued another, more emphatic declination, which made it less likely that he could honorably bow to a draft, but many of his supporters still clung to their dream of swinging the convention his way.

The initial balloting at the Republican convention in Chicago showed a wide dispersal of votes for several candidates, which augured well for the Blaine strategy. Yet as the voting dragged on over several days, it became clear that Sherman and some other candidates would never withdraw in Blaine's favor, and there would be no unanimous demand for the Plumed Knight. Meanwhile, Harrison's managers gradually picked up delegates, many from the Blaine camp. In huddling with other state delegations, they pointed out that Harrison had garnered the vast majority of the votes of New York, Indiana, New Jersey, and Connecticut, the four northern doubtful states vital to the party's chances in November. With the Blaine strategy unraveling, a third and final refusal arrived from the non-candidate, and the movement toward Harrison ended with his nomination on the eighth ballot. For vice president, the convention chose a member of the old New York Stalwart wing, Levi P. Morton, a wealthy banker who could help bankroll the campaign.

The platform took direct aim at the Democrats on the tariff issue. "We are uncompromisingly in favor of the American system of protection," it declared, and "we protest against its destruction as proposed by the President and his party." The document "denounce[d] the Mills bill as destructive to the general business, the labor, and the farming interests of the country." To cut the surplus, the Republicans favored cutting taxes on tobacco and revising customs duties upward to "check imports" and thus reduce revenue. If necessary, they favored "the entire repeal of internal revenue taxes rather than the surrender of any part of our protective system." They were also willing to reduce the surplus through increased spending for such purposes as aid to education, defense, internal improvements, and pensions for veterans. Bowing to the wishes of the silver-producing West, the party endorsed both gold and silver as money and condemned Cleveland for trying to demonetize silver. On civil rights and the southern question, the platform demanded "effective legislation to secure the integrity and purity of elections" and charged that the Democrats held the House of Representatives and the White House as a result of "the suppression of the ballot by a criminal nullification of the Constitution and laws of the United States."[21]

The tariff issue dominated the fall campaign. The only substantive statement Cleveland made on the issue came in his formal letter of acceptance. Once again he tried to deflect the criticism raised against his tariff message and the Mills bill. Tariff revenues should be limited to "the necessities of a frugal and economical" government, but, he insisted, "we have entered upon no crusade of free trade." Instead, he promised "the utmost care for established industries and enterprises" and disavowed any "abrupt and radical changes which might endanger such enterprises and injuriously affect the interests of labor." Some protectionist Democrats remained unconvinced by the president's declarations. When Samuel Randall refused to campaign for the ticket, he pleaded ill health, but he also told the national campaign chairman, "I do not propose to take back any of my utterances, the result of conviction, on the tariff."[22]

Republicans scoffed at the president's attempt to pull back on the issue. "It is the same old story," declared one congressman. "It is like the dentist who says he is not going to hurt while he is pulling your tooth." Harrison also emphasized the tariff question in his letter of acceptance. He defended protectionism as "constitutional, wholesome and necessary." "We believe it to be one of the worthy objects of tariff legislation to preserve the American market for American producers, and to maintain the American scale of wages." If the Democrats had their way, he wrote, they would put the tariff laws on "a purely revenue basis. This is practical free trade, free trade in the English sense." Harrison denied that reduction of the surplus would require repeal of all internal taxes, thereby hoping to reassure temperance voters that the Republicans' program did not call for tax-free whiskey. For the burgeoning revenues, Harrison envisioned worthwhile uses such as aid to education, increased veterans' pensions, and reduction of the national debt.[23]

In the general campaign, Harrison did not want to forgo speaking as Cleveland did, but he did not wish to travel and risk the sort of mistakes that had marred the end of Blaine's 1884 tour. Instead, he remained in Indianapolis and spoke to visiting delegations that

A Republican campaign poster emphasizes the party's policy of protection for industry, labor, and farmers. (Library of Congress)

came to him. In a highly effective front-porch campaign, his managers day after day orchestrated the visits of several groups of voters, and to each one the candidate delivered a short address geared to the interests of the visitors. His own stenographer recorded his words and provided them to the Associated Press, through which they appeared in hundreds of newspapers across the country. Harrison enjoyed the comfort of his own home but reached millions of voters nearly every day. In these talks he again stressed tariff protectionism. In the early fall, the Republican Senate produced a countermeasure to the Mills bill and thus provided Harrison and other Republican campaigners another text upon which to base their protectionist appeals.

By 1888 the southern question had been reduced to a secondary concern in national political discourse. Harrison occasionally called attention to the violation of voting rights in the South, noting that he was unwilling "to purchase the Presidency by a compact of silence upon this question." Like Blaine, Harrison hoped to use economic appeals to dislodge states from the Solid South and reduce Republican dependence on northern doubtful states, but he also sought to combine the economic and voting rights issues. He urged southerners who agreed with the GOP's protectionist stand not only to "throw off old prejudices and vote their convictions upon that question" but also to insist that blacks and white Republicans "who believe with them shall vote, and that their votes shall be counted." Protecting the right to vote, he insisted, would provide protection for southern economic interests.[24]

For their part, Cleveland and the Democrats paid lip service to the ideal of equal rights, but their greater concern was maintaining their base in the white South. They denounced Harrison as a "bitter, unscrupulous, malignant hater of the South," as Indiana Democratic senator Daniel Voorhees told a North Carolina audience. When Democrats spoke of the ideal of sectional reconciliation, they signaled to white southerners their intention that the federal government should take no effective action to alter the social system in the region. They tacitly upheld the racial order in the South and even moved to squelch a rumor that Cleveland had invited the African American leader Frederick Douglass to the White House. Democrats, like Republicans, tried to combine sectional and economic issues. They warned southerners that if the Republicans gained control of the federal government, they aimed to revive Reconstruction with "new repressive legislation," setting off "a panic in the South" that would "injure credit, disorganize industry and stop development."[25]

Foreign affairs figured in the campaign less as a question of national security than as a vehicle for arousing voters' ethnic animosities. Both Harrison and Cleveland appealed to white voters on the West Coast by vehemently opposing the immigration of Chinese labor. Each party accused the other of truckling under to the British in a dispute related to American fishing rights in Canadian waters. In the summer, Cleveland scored points with a bombastic message to Congress demanding retaliatory powers to deal with the question. Toward the end of the campaign, however, he fell victim to a ruse that a California Republican played on the British minister in Washington. Posing as a former British subject, the Californian asked which candidate would be better for British interests, and the minister's fatuous reply favoring Cleveland was given to the press. An outraged Cleveland threw the minister out of the country, but the incident may have hurt the president's chances, particularly among Irish Americans.

As was usual in this period, the end of the campaign witnessed a barrage of charges and countercharges of contemplated fraud, especially in the doubtful states. In Indiana, Republicans published a circular in which a Democratic county chairman allegedly instructed party workers in vote-buying techniques. The Democrats countered by publishing a similar letter purportedly from the Republican national treasurer, William W. Dudley, himself a Hoosier, urging Indiana campaign workers to organize the purchasable "floating" voters into "blocks of five" to get them to the polls.[26] The impact, and even the existence, of such schemes remain murky. Neither party was entirely innocent, and their efforts may well have canceled each other. The more significant fraud in 1888 occurred in the South, with the continued widespread suppression of the African American vote.

On election day, largely because of that suppression, Cleveland rolled up huge margins in several Deep South states, allowing him to surpass Harrison in the nationwide tally by more than 90,000 votes. Yet Harrison won New York and Indiana and defeated the president in the electoral college by a vote of 233 to 168. Harrison squeaked past Cleveland by 1.1 percent in New York and 0.4 percent in Indiana. The election had not broken the equilibrium in American politics, nor had it substantially reconfigured the sectional character of party strength. Cleveland carried all the old slave states plus Connecticut and New Jersey; Harrison won all the other states outside of the South. In the South, Cleveland ran ahead of Harrison by 563,869 votes; in the rest of the nation, where voting was largely unrestrained, Harrison's margin over Cleveland stood at 473,273. But even though sectional voting patterns persisted, most postelection observers attributed the outcome to the tariff issue. Republicans considered it an endorsement of the protectionism they had espoused, while Democrats who agreed with Cleveland lamented that time had been lacking to convince voters of the need for the changes he had outlined. Protectionist Democrats thought that the result simply confirmed their prophecy that the president's course would defeat the party and endanger the nation.

Harrison's southern tariff strategy came near to bearing fruit in the Upper South, where the growth of various industries made the Republicans' economic arguments more appealing. In Virginia he collected 49.5 percent of the vote, a share greater than he received in either New York or his home state of Indiana. In addition, he received 49 percent in West Virginia, 47.4 percent in Maryland, 47.1 percent in North Carolina, and 45.8 percent in Tennessee. Moreover, the Republicans gained nine congressional seats in the South, bringing the total of southern Republican representatives to twenty-five. With gains elsewhere, the GOP won a majority in the House. In the Senate they retained their majority, which grew substantially in the new Congress with the admission of six new western states to the Union.

Although the election of 1888 did not result in a permanent shift in the party balance in the country, it did end with the Republicans in clear control of the White House, the Senate, and the House of Representatives for the first time in a decade and a half. "It gives you," a jubilant James G. Blaine wrote President-elect Harrison, "the amplest power for a useful, strong and impressive Administration."[27] After years of stalemate in Washington, Republicans were at last once again in a position to act.

FIVE

Harrison, Cleveland, and the Purposes of Power

In the wake of his defeat, Grover Cleveland turned to preparing his last annual message, in which he presented a bitter indictment of conditions in American society. Cleveland described the country as under threat from a pervasive combination of "wealth and capital, the outgrowth of overweening cupidity and selfishness, which insidiously undermines the justice and integrity of free institutions." Although he did not explicitly blame his election loss on such forces, he asserted that they did "improperly influence the suffrages of the people." More broadly, he decried the rapid division of the nation into classes, "one comprising the very rich and powerful, while in another are found the toiling poor." At the same time that "aggregated capital" enjoyed "the discriminating favor of the Government," he said, the average citizen "is struggling far in the rear or is trampled to death beneath an iron heel."

Yet the solution that Cleveland prescribed for this dire state echoed the essentially negative message of his campaign. Again he called for a reduction of the tariff to lift "undue exactions from the masses of our people." Less, not more, government was the answer to the nation's troubles. "Extravagant appropriations of public money, with all their demoralizing consequences, should not be tolerated." The president urged Americans to repudiate "the sentiment largely prevailing among the people that the General Government is the fountain of individual and private aid." They should reject the expansion of "Federal legislation into the domain of State and local jurisdiction upon the plea of subserving the public welfare." Instead, "a just and sensible revision of our tariff laws should be made for the relief of those of our countrymen who suffer under present conditions."[1]

The Republicans soon to assume power may have seen some truth in Cleveland's depiction of the nation's ills, but they denied the efficacy of his laissez-faire nostrum. In his inaugural address, Benjamin Harrison put the country on notice that the Republican administration and Congress would pursue a more activist agenda. The new president pointed to the indispensability of the protective tariff for "the preservation and development of domestic industries and the defense of our working people." He assured southerners that they too could share in the bounty of tariff protection, and he exhorted them not to let "the prejudices and paralysis of slavery continue to hang upon the skirts of progress." He urged southern whites interested in economic development to "make the black man their efficient and safe ally." If they did not, he warned, "no power vested in Congress or in the Executive to secure or perpetuate" the "freedom of the ballot" should "remain unused." Describing the Treasury surplus as "serious" but "not the greatest evil," he insisted that "nothing in the condition of our country" suggested that useful spending "should be unduly postponed." He advocated expenditures to expand the navy, subsidize American steamship lines, and increase veterans' pensions. Celebrating the positive uses of government, Harrison embraced a ruling credo affirming that "justice and mercy shall hold the reins of power and that the upward avenues of hope shall be free to all the people."[2] In his first annual message in December 1889 the president elaborated these themes and added calls for spending on coastal defenses, internal improvements, and aid to education, as well as new legislation to settle the silver question and to institute punitive measures against the trusts.

The Republicans in Congress responded, launching one of the most fruitful legislative sessions in history. Democrats in the House initially resorted to a variety of obstructionist maneuvers to block their efforts, but Speaker Thomas B. Reed instituted new rules that overrode these dilatory tactics. Like Harrison, Reed believed that the "danger in a free country is not that power will be exercised too freely, but that it will be exercised too sparingly."[3] Although Democrats labeled the Speaker "Czar" Reed, his rules allowed the majority to proceed with its agenda. At the top of the list was the tariff, which was debated off and on throughout the session until the approval of the McKinley Tariff Act in early October 1890. The act bore the name of its principal author, Ways and Means chairman William McKinley, but both Harrison and Secretary of State James G. Blaine played crucial roles in shaping it and squiring it to passage.

The complex law was designed to achieve two goals: preserve protection and reduce the surplus. It reduced or eliminated customs duties on many items, especially ones that did not compete with American production. Among the items it placed on the free list was sugar, a move designed to appeal to consumers worried about high prices. Moreover, because sugar duties had generated a large portion of tariff revenue (about $55 million), eliminating those duties would help cut the surplus. The act also called for a bounty of two cents per pound to American sugar producers to compensate for their loss of tariff protection; payment of the bounty would further reduce the surplus. To fulfill the protective purpose, the act raised rates sharply on many items, to an overall average of 49.5 percent, a record for peacetime. Some duties reached levels that discouraged importation altogether, thereby not only providing protection but also cutting the revenues.

To ward off the indignation of farmers irritated by the high costs of manufactures, the act raised customs duties on a variety of farm products, many such imports being taxed for the first time. More important for farmers, the act empowered the president to negotiate reciprocity agreements with foreign nations, which would open up markets for American agricultural products, especially in Latin America. Before leaving office, Harrison sealed such agreements with more than ten countries, to which American exports rose by 20 percent. (Also for the benefit of farmers, Congress passed the Meat Inspection Act, which helped reopen foreign markets for American pork products.) Republican strategists portrayed the McKinley Act as offering something for everyone: industrialists, labor, farmers, and consumers.

Republicans hoped to appeal to an equally broad spectrum in dealing with the silver question. Democratic divisions during the Cleveland years had prevented either abolishing the limited coinage under the Bland-Allison Act of 1878 or establishing free coinage. Republicans showed similar divisions, but Harrison and other party leaders were determined to strike some sort of accommodation that would resolve the question at least temporarily and diminish its political liabilities. The issue had grown more pressing in the late 1880s with the spread of economic troubles in the agricultural regions of the West and South. Farmers in debt and others who had difficulty meeting their obligations looked to free coinage of silver as a way to expand the money supply and make their financial burdens less onerous. Groups such as the Farmers' Alliance had sprung up and undermined allegiances to the two major parties. Silver interests in the Far West naturally favored increased government purchase of their product. But creditors fearful of being paid in cheap, debased money insisted that only the preservation of the gold standard would ensure "honest money" for the nation. The Indiana Republican chairman reminded the administration that the Alliance had endorsed free silver and warned that failure to pass "very wise legislation" would mean "disaster to the Republican party."[4]

After prolonged debate, Republicans led by John Sherman hammered out a compromise, passed in July 1890. The Sherman Silver Purchase Act called for the Treasury to purchase 4.5 million ounces of the metal per month, virtually the entire output of American mines. Instead of coining the silver, however, the government would issue certificates against it to be used as currency, and the act gave the Treasury the authority to redeem these certificates in gold or its equivalent. Not a single Democrat in either house voted for the final measure. Republicans hoped it would appeal to inflationists favoring increased use of silver, silver mine interests, and hard-money forces of the East who clung to the gold standard. Harrison had lobbied strenuously for an acceptable bill, and although the Sherman Act was not precisely what he wanted, he was "glad to end a controversy by signing it."[5]

Sherman lent his name to another landmark law, this one dealing with the problem of monopoly. Both major parties had called for such legislation during the campaign of 1888. In August of that year, the Ohio senator had introduced an antitrust bill, and the new Fifty-first Congress renewed consideration of the subject. The bill attracted bipartisan support, and others joined Sherman in working out its final version. As passed, the Sherman Antitrust Act outlawed combinations, trusts, contracts, and conspiracies in restraint of trade or commerce. Although the act was narrower than Sherman's original bill, subsequent legislation and court decisions broadened its scope and refined its application. The act, passed in July 1890, laid down the principles of American antimonopoly policy that persist to this day.

With these laws, the Republicans were laying the foundation for a new economic order, with tariff protection to stimulate American production, reciprocity to expand exports, a balanced but growing money supply to meet the economy's needs, and government regulation to counter monopolistic tendencies. The Republicans' governing formula also contemplated liberal expenditures. The Fifty-first Congress made generous appropriations for internal improvements, coastal defenses, and expansion of the navy. During the 1888 campaign Harrison had made special appeal to his fellow Union

The National Grab-Bag. *Puck* assails the expenditures of President Benjamin Harrison and the Republican Fifty-first Congress. (*Puck*, April 16, 1890)

veterans, so he took particular pleasure in signing the Dependent Pension Act, embodying the principles Cleveland had vetoed. The act granted a pension of $12 per month to an invalid veteran or, if he had died, to his surviving dependents. By the end of Harrison's term, pension expenditures had climbed to 40 percent of the government's receipts and thus contributed to a reduction in the surplus. Modern scholars regard the 1890 Pension Act as a milestone in the development of American welfare policy.

Republicans also undertook another piece of legislation that had a distinctly modern ring to it: a bill to protect voting rights. The election of 1888 had at last given the Republicans the first real opportunity since Ulysses S. Grant's term to do something about the southern question, and the results of that election in the Deep South underscored the need. In the three black majority states of Louisiana, Mississippi, and South Carolina, for instance, tallies conducted by Democratic state and local officials had given Harrison substantially less than 30 percent of the vote; in South Carolina, where African Americans constituted 60 percent of the citizenry, only 17.2 percent of the vote was counted for Harrison. Congressional elections showed similar lopsided results. After the election, the urgency of the situation received startling reinforcement with the cold-blooded murder of a Republican congressional candidate in Arkansas who was investigating the theft of a ballot box that had led to his defeat. "When and under what conditions is the black man to have a free ballot?" Harrison demanded in his first annual message. "This generation should courageously face these grave questions, and not leave them as a heritage of woe to the next."[6]

Congressional Republicans responded with the Lodge Federal Elections bill, named for House Elections Committee chairman Henry Cabot Lodge. Applying only to congressional elections, the measure called for federal oversight, not takeover, of suspect elections. At the request of a body of citizens, a federal judge could appoint supervisors to monitor the registering of voters, the conduct of elections, and the counting of votes. Along with the vote tallies that state officials made, the supervisors would report their tabulations to a federal board of canvassers who would decide which candidate won. If the canvassers' decision came under challenge, a federal judge would make the determination.

What most alarmed white southerners and their northern Democratic allies was that election decisions that—since the end of Reconstruction—had rested in the hands of Democratic state and local officials would now, under the bill, become the province of federal canvassers and judges who were likely to be Republicans. Such a system had the potential to rework the lines of power and control in the South, with consequences for national governance as well. Should black Republicans in the South gain their constitutional right to vote, the equilibrium in national politics might well tip in favor of the GOP.

Democrats put up a fierce opposition, calling the Lodge measure a "force bill." They warned that passage would revive Reconstruction and install armed soldiers at southern polling places to ensure Republican victory. Republicans responded that the purpose was to end violence and intimidation and to place responsibility for fair elections in the hands of the courts, not the military. With Speaker Reed in firm command of procedures, the House passed the bill by a party vote of 155 to 149 on July 2, 1890.

Senate rules did not lend themselves to such expedition and control by the majority. To make the bill more palatable, Senate Republicans excised a reference to the president's authority to use troops to uphold the law and added a stipulation that recognized the power of the House of Representatives to reverse a judge's decision regarding a member's election. Democrats were unmoved, however, and during the summer they adopted the tactic of dragging out the debate on the McKinley Tariff bill indefinitely in order to prevent the Senate from moving on to the Lodge bill. Republicans could not muster enough votes to change the rules to limit debate, and some Republicans who placed a higher priority on tariff legislation began to suggest that the elections bill be shelved. After heated debates in caucus, the Republicans reached an agreement to put the Lodge bill off until the Congress's second session in December and to proceed with the tariff deliberations. Senate backers of the Lodge bill expressed their conviction that it would prevail in the second session, but some observers were not so sure. As Frederick Douglass asked a senator, "What if we gain the tariff and many other good things if in doing it the soul of the party and nation is lost?"[7]

After one of the longest and most productive sessions in its history, Congress adjourned on October 1, 1890, scarcely a month before the Republicans would test the voters' reaction in the midterm congressional elections. Democrats lost no time in damning what the GOP had wrought. The McKinley Tariff, they charged, would nourish trusts and send prices through the roof, while the Lodge bill threatened to bludgeon democracy. Taking aim at the increased expenditures, Democrats condemned what they called the Billion Dollar Congress. Reed responded that it was "a Billion Dollar Country," but the Democrats nonetheless sharpened their appeals to the long-standing American suspicion of activist government. Democrats also fine-tuned their alarmist message at the state level in some midwestern states where certain ethnic groups reacted against Republican-sponsored temperance legislation or laws requiring that immigrant schools teach in the English language. Moreover, many of the nation's farmers thought that the new tariff favored eastern manufacturers at their expense and that the new silver legislation was wholly inadequate to meet the country's currency needs. A severe money stringency in mid-September, just as crop-moving season was beginning, had heightened farmers' anxieties. By that time the Farmers' Alliance claimed more than a million members, and Republicans feared large defections to third parties, especially in the Midwest. In October, President Harrison took a speaking tour through the endangered region, warning farmers not to fall for "unsafe expedients."[8]

Harrison's effort proved of little avail, for Republicans lost overwhelmingly in the November election. In the new national House, the Republicans garnered only 88 seats to the Democrats' 235. The GOP lost nearly everywhere. In the South the party's representation fell from twenty-five to four. In New England, New Hampshire elected two Democrats and no Republicans; Massachusetts, seven Democrats and five Republicans; and Connecticut, three Democrats and one Republican. The Democrats would dominate the delegations of five key midwestern states by fifty-five seats to nineteen. In the normally Republican, trans-Mississippi agricultural states, the party's fortunes similarly declined. Nebraska elected two members from the People's Party, the political arm of the farmers' movement, plus Democrat Williams Jennings Bryan. In Kansas, five of seven congressional seats went to Populists, and the Populist state legislature elected one of their party to the Senate. Minnesota voters chose three Democrats and a Populist for the national House, and one lone Republican. Even in Iowa the Democrats won six of eleven House seats. Beyond those who openly wore the People's Party label, more than forty members of the new House, a great many of them from the South, had won election with the support of the Farmers' Alliance.

Observers attributed the outcome to a variety of influences, the McKinley Tariff Act among the most important. Democrats effectively employed the high-price scare, even to the point of paying itinerant peddlers to jack up their prices on housewares made of tin, on which the McKinley Act had raised rates to prohibitive levels. Meanwhile, the price of sugar remained high because, under the terms of the act, it would not go on the free list until April 1891. From Indiana, Harrison's chief political adviser reported that of "the men who contributed to our defeat . . . about nine-tenths of them were out of humor with the McKinley bill." Harrison was reluctant to place all blame on the tariff, because the returns showed that the Republicans had run well in some states with protected interests and had suffered defeat in others. He saw other forces at work, such

"NAPOLEON'S RETREAT."

After the congressional elections of 1890, William McKinley, the "Napoleon of Protection," leads the defeated Republicans in retreat. (*Puck*, November 19, 1890)

as reaction against the English-language school law in Wisconsin. He worried about the future impact of the farmers' movements on such states as Kansas and Nebraska, but he also took comfort in the belief that "all such secret organizations are . . . shortlived." He considered much of the disaffection from the Republicans only temporary, and he conceded that some state party leaders had been put off by his own failure to fulfill their patronage requests. Most important, the president did "not believe the Democratic party has grown in the confidence of the country, nor been augmented by any permanent accessions."[9]

Democrats, of course, optimistically believed otherwise. Even though the Republicans would retain control of the Senate in the Fifty-second Congress, hopeful Democrats viewed the House elections of 1890 as the seismic shift they had been waiting for to break the national equilibrium. According to Kentucky senator John G. Carlisle, the American people had unequivocally rejected the "radical and revolutionary policy" the Republican Party had pursued since "it found itself in complete control of the government." A gleeful Grover Cleveland hailed the "tremendous" Democratic victory as "the triumph of the doctrines we have struggled for."[10]

The emboldened Democrats, even though still in the minority in the second session of the Fifty-first Congress, were determined to block passage of the Lodge Elections bill. In the Senate they conducted a prolonged filibuster against the bill. Convinced that the recent election amounted to a public condemnation of the measure, they vowed not to allow the Republicans to "warm the cold fingers of this cadaver at the dying embers of sectional hatred." In the end, the bill fell victim to an understanding between a handful of western state pro-silver Republicans, who agreed to vote against the Lodge bill, and Democrats, who agreed to back consideration of free coinage of silver. As a leading silver Republican senator put it, "there are many things more important and vital to the welfare of this nation than that the colored citizens of the South shall vote."

The bill's defeat profoundly dismayed its backers, for as one Republican senator sadly wrote, "The Lord only knows when, if ever, we shall have another chance to pass an election bill." Indeed, the Lodge bill turned out to be the last significant attempt at civil rights legislation until the middle of the twentieth century. Ironically, partly in reaction to the Lodge bill, Democrats in the southern states began instituting "legal" suppression of the African American vote through such means as poll taxes, literacy tests, and the grandfather clause.[11]

Although they failed to secure passage of the Elections bill, Harrison and his congressional allies won a few more victories before the second session expired. Republicans in the House managed to kill the free coinage bill passed by the Senate. Congress passed a postal subsidy bill under which the government would pay steamship lines to carry mail overseas, with the broader aim of reviving the American carrying trade and aiding the expansion of commerce. And as the session drew to a close, Harrison successfully pushed for the Forest Reserve Act, which empowered the president to set aside federal land for national forests. Anticipating the conservation movement of the early twentieth century, Harrison designated thirteen million acres as forest reserves.

By March 1891 the Republicans could look back at the Fifty-first Congress as one of remarkable accomplishment. It had passed 531 public laws, a record unequaled until Theodore Roosevelt's second term. Henry Cabot Lodge, who held a Ph.D. and had taught history at Harvard University, wrote that "no Congress in peace time since the first has passed so many great & important measures of lasting value to the people." Harrison called it "a most remarkable Congress" whose work was "of the most important character." He could justly take a measure of the credit, for he had played a key role in the legislative process, both through public pronouncements and in behind-the-scenes lobbying and negotiation. As one observer noted, Harrison as president exhibited "higher views of the functions of administration than the beaten path of routine and precedent." His actions would provide important lessons for presidents to come.[12]

Yet for all he achieved in his dealing with Congress, Harrison proved far less successful as the leader of his party. Never a backslapping politician, he had risen to prominence on the strength of his intellect rather than the warmth of his personality. Harrison was the first Republican president to take over from a Democrat since Abraham Lincoln succeeded James Buchanan in 1861. Like Cleveland before him, Harrison confronted a hungry host of party cadres eager for patronage recognition for helping to get him elected. And like Cleveland, he did not have nearly enough offices to reward all the supplicants. His administration had hardly begun before the disappointed began to grumble about his ingratitude and coldness. Many of them began to pine for the warmth and magnetism of James G. Blaine, whom Harrison had appointed secretary of state.

Within the cabinet, the relationship between the two men started out cordially but soon deteriorated. Blaine could not shake the notion that he had made Harrison president, and he relished being depicted in the press as the "premier" of the administration. Carrying Republican activism into foreign affairs, the team posted some notable achievements: the Berlin Condominium with Britain and Germany to manage the island nation of Samoa, the Pan-American Conference with representatives of the Western Hemisphere, reciprocity agreements to expand trade, and an agreement with Britain to submit to arbitration a controversy over the hunting of fur seals in the Bering Sea. Yet Blaine was ill much of the time, and he spent long periods at his seaside home in Maine while Harrison labored over diplomatic questions in Washington, nursing a growing and justified resentment. By the spring of 1892 their communication had been reduced almost exclusively to exchanging letters and notes, even when Blaine was in the capital.

By that time, also, the jockeying was well under way for the party's presidential nomination. As early as mid-1891, many Republicans who had grown disenchanted with Harrison indicated their preference for Blaine, who, as in 1888, hinted that he might be interested if the party were solidly for him. The Blaine maneuvers did not catch the Harrison camp unawares. The president and his allies began more pointedly to exercise the prerogatives of incumbency to exert control over the party organization, such that in early February 1892 Blaine announced that he was not a candidate. Yet true to form, Blaine did not issue an outright refusal of a draft, and his supporters, led by New Yorker Thomas Platt and former national chairman Matthew Quay, continued to push him. So also did his wife, who hated Harrison for refusing to give her son a preferred position in the State Department as his father's chief assistant. In late May, Blaine ostentatiously visited New York, where Platt privately pleaded with him to run. The following week, on the eve of the national convention, Blaine resigned from the cabinet. It proved a tragic end to the secretary's otherwise distinguished career. In deeply precarious health, he allowed himself to be used by others for their own selfish ends and incurred certain defeat. The Harrison forces managed to command the Minneapolis convention and on a single ballot defeated Blaine and a dark horse candidacy by William McKinley. In a feint toward party unity, the convention gave the vice presidential nomination to *New York Tribune* proprietor Whitelaw Reid, long known as one of Blaine's strongest backers.

The platform gave primacy of place to the protective tariff and claimed that "the prosperous condition of our country is largely due to the wise revenue legislation of the Republican Congress." It condemned recent efforts by the Democratic House to reduce or remove duties on several items. The party favored the use of both gold and silver as money, as long as the ratio was adjusted to ensure the parity of their value. The chairman of the platform committee, Joseph B. Foraker, an ardent defender of black rights, inserted a strong plank on the southern question, decrying "the continued inhuman outrages" against citizens in the South and pledging that the party would "never relax its efforts until the integrity of the ballot and the purity of elections shall be fully guaranteed and protected in every State." This plank did not much worry the Democrats, who believed that the push for the Lodge bill had turned opinion against the Republicans on civil rights issues. Only in its last plank did the platform offer a mild commendation of "the able, patriotic and thoroughly American administration of President Harrison."[13]

The Democrats approached the election of 1892 confident that the tide was with them. Party members who interpreted the election of 1890 as an endorsement of their low-tariff philosophy naturally favored another nomination for its leading champion, Grover Cleveland. Out of office, Cleveland did not discourage the speculation, making a number of well-received speeches attacking the handiwork of the Fifty-first Congress, especially the McKinley Act. Cleveland still opposed free coinage, but he hoped to keep that party-rending issue in the background. As in 1888, David B. Hill put up a challenge to Cleveland and even managed to capture the New York delegation, but his candidacy attracted little support elsewhere, while the Cleveland juggernaut rolled through the rest of the country collecting delegates. At the national convention in Chicago, the former president won his third nomination on the first ballot.

As in 1888, however, Cleveland encountered trouble in attempting to moderate the convention's stand on the tariff issue. His representatives in Chicago, former members of his cabinet William C. Whitney and William F. Vilas, proposed a plank that borrowed language verbatim from the "straddle" platform of 1884, balancing a call for tariff reduction with the recognition that any change "must be at every step regardful of the labor and capital thus involved." Low-tariff advocates, under the leadership of Kentuckian Henry Watterson, objected in the platform committee and, after losing there, carried their fight to the convention floor. They proposed a substitute plank that denounced "Republican protection as a fraud" and declared that the government had "no constitutional power to impose and collect tariff duties except for the purposes of revenue only." On a roll call vote, the substitute prevailed handily, and Cleveland was livid. He wrote Whitney that Watterson had "from pure cussedness, put this plank in the platform, which is going to make us more trouble than anything else in the campaign." More to the nominee's liking, the convention adopted a money plank labeling the Sherman Silver Act a "cowardly makeshift" and favoring the use of both gold and silver, as long as they were maintained at equal value, and it easily beat back an amendment for free coinage. To mollify the silverites, the convention gave the vice presidential nomination to one of them, Adlai E. Stevenson of Illinois, who also appealed to party regulars as the dispenser of post office patronage during Cleveland's first term in the White House.[14]

The Democrats took direct aim at the Lodge Elections bill, which they called the Force bill, as "fraught with the gravest dangers, scarcely less momentous than would result from a revolution practically establishing monarchy on the ruins of the republic."[15] Despite the strong civil rights language of their platform, Republicans showed little inclination to defend the Lodge bill, but Democrats still harped on it, primarily to appeal to their base in the South, where they perceived a menacing threat from the Populists.

The Populist movement had gained momentum in a series of meetings that drew representatives of both farmers and laborers, and the People's Party had emerged as a national entity at a conference in St. Louis in February 1892. Five months later, the new party held a convention in Omaha and nominated for president former Iowa congressman James B. Weaver, who had headed the Greenback ticket in 1880. To balance the former Union general, the convention chose for vice president James G. Field, a Confederate veteran and former Democrat from Virginia.

The Populist platform portrayed the new party as the champion of all working people, rural and urban. Its preamble was written by

Ignatius Donnelly, a former Republican congressman from Minnesota and sometime novelist who did not confine his flights of fancy to his literary efforts. In an apocalyptic tone, Donnelly asserted that the nation was on "the verge of moral, political and material ruin" and that "governmental injustice" was breeding "two great classes—tramps and millionaires." He dismissed the two major parties as using the "uproar of a sham battle over the tariff" to gull the people while the politicians struggled for "power and plunder." As steps to alleviate these grave conditions, the Populist platform proposed free and unlimited coinage of silver at a ratio of sixteen to one with gold, a graduated income tax, and government ownership of the railroads and the telegraph and telephone systems.[16]

Neither the Democrats nor the Republicans accepted the Populists' notion that their tariff differences represented a sham battle. Nor it seems did Americans generally, as evinced by the high turnout rates in elections when the issue was the center of discussion or by the volume of mail relating to the tariff that party leaders received from ordinary citizens. The importance of the issue was clear when, just about the time the Populists met in Omaha, the Republican argument for protection received a major setback owing to labor strife at Andrew Carnegie's steel works at Homestead, Pennsylvania. Substantial wage cuts had sparked a strike by the plant's workers, who were then locked out by manager Henry Clay Frick. When Frick hired a Pinkerton squad to clear the way for strikebreakers, armed fighting ensued, leaving thirteen men dead. The Republicans dispatched an associate of Whitelaw Reid to try to convince Frick to negotiate with the workers, but he refused, and the Pennsylvania militia eventually put down the strike.

The incident was doubly damaging to the Republicans. Not only did Carnegie have close ties to party leaders, but, more important, Republicans had long pointed to steel industry workers as prime beneficiaries of protectionism. The events at Homestead argued otherwise. The reproach was compounded by other labor troubles in the

silver mines of Idaho, the coal mines of Tennessee, the rail yards of
Buffalo, and even the printing plant of Reid's *New York Tribune*. In a
rare public appearance to acknowledge his nomination, Cleveland
savored the Republicans' discomfiture over Homestead, telling a
crowd at Madison Square Garden, "Scenes are enacted in the very
abiding place of high protection that mock the hopes of toil." Such
scenes showed workers the "demonstrated falsity that the existing
protective tariff is a boon to them."[17]

Cleveland said little else publicly during the campaign except
for his official letter of acceptance in late September. Believing that
the Republicans were now more vulnerable on the tariff, he was less
inclined to temper the Democrats' position. Despite his anger at the
radicalism of Watterson's platform plank in July, his letter, like that
plank, decried a tariff for protection as "clearly contrary to the spirit
of our Constitution," a position that echoed that of John C. Calhoun
sixty years earlier. Espousing the notions of classical political economy, he described the "especial purpose and mission of our free
Government" as guarding "the people in the exclusive use and enjoyment of their property and earnings." A tariff for protection rather
than simply for necessary revenue, he insisted, represented "a diminution of the property rights of the people." "Paternalism in government," he avowed, "finds no approval in the creed of Democracy. It
is a symptom of misrule." With no sense of irony regarding the
Democrats' suppression of the black vote in the South, Cleveland
suggested that the Lodge Elections bill reflected the Republicans'
"reckless disregard of a free expression of the popular will."[18]

As the incumbent, Harrison naturally used his letter of acceptance, about three times as long as Cleveland's, to offer a detailed
defense of what his administration had wrought. He aimed his appeal primarily at farmers and workers, asserting that the "general
condition of our country is one of great prosperity." Citing a raft of
figures compiled by a bipartisan Senate committee and by the
Democratic chief of New York State's Bureau of Labor Statistics, he

ascribed great benefits to the McKinley Tariff, not only in its protective features but in its reciprocity clause as well. Wages had risen, farm prices had gone up, foreign markets for farm commodities had expanded, and the prices the average working family paid on household articles had declined. With a particular eye to farmers tempted by Populism, Harrison hailed the expansion of overseas sales of their goods, thanks to reciprocity. "Are the farmers of the great grain-growing States," he asked, "willing to surrender these new, large and increasing markets for their surplus?" The Democrats, he warned, would kill the reciprocity program as well as launch a "mad crusade against American shops." Enactment of Cleveland's tariff ideas would "at once plunge the nation into a business convulsion such as it has never seen." On the money question, Harrison stated that he favored "the free coinage of silver," thus employing the talismanic phrase in hopes of appealing to inflationist farmers. But he also added "the one essential condition" that gold and silver dollars must "retain an equal acceptability and value."[19]

On the southern question, Harrison called for a free ballot and a fair count, but he did not mention the Lodge bill. Instead, he repeated a call in his latest annual message for a nonpartisan commission to study the elections question. Moreover, Harrison tried to appeal to Populists in the South on the issue by noting that they, like the Republicans, were victims of white Democratic frauds. He pointed to the recent state election in Alabama in which Democrats manipulated the vote in black counties to defeat a Republican-Populist fusion candidate for governor. Despite this setback, he urged "these new political movements" to help correct "the arbitrary and partisan election laws and practices" in the region. Other Republicans were equally circumspect on the issue. The Republican campaign textbook briefly summarized the Lodge bill but asserted that it contained "not a line or a word suggest[ing] Federal bayonets" and was "no more a 'Force Bill' than are the Ten Commandments." The textbook added that the party was "in no sense committed to this bill, or to any other particular method of curing the evil of dishonest elections." Indeed, admitting defeat on the issue, Republicans had come to recognize that they could not rally public opinion behind federal action to defend voting rights in the South.[20]

Democrats, for their part, refused to admit victory on the issue. They continued to raise the specter of Republican-sponsored "negro domination." Cleveland himself lashed out against the "Force Bill" as not only "a most atrocious measure" but "a direct attack upon the spirit and theory of our Government."[21]

The Democrats played upon sectional and racial animosity primarily in order to keep whites in the South united in the face of the Populist challenge. James Weaver, the Populist nominee, was an experienced campaigner and hoped that a personal speaking tour would convince destitute southern farmers to abandon their Democratic allegiance and vote their economic interest. Yet in the initial phase of his tour in Georgia, wherever Weaver went, Democratic rowdies and ruffians showed up to disrupt his speeches by heckling, throwing things, or worse. Nor did the presence of Weaver's wife or the noted Kansas woman orator, Mary E. Lease, on the platform subdue the disorders. At Macon, a mob tossed rotten eggs, tomatoes, and rocks at the threesome, driving Mrs. Lease to observe that "Mrs. Weaver was made a regular walking omelet by the southern chivalry of Georgia."[22] Weaver moved on to the Carolinas, Virginia, and Tennessee, where he was allowed to speak, but the determination of the Democrats to hang on to power at whatever cost was clear. Night riders, a tradition in southern politics since Reconstruction, now turned their violence and intimidation against Populists and their sympathizers. Weaver encountered a much more congenial atmosphere when he turned his campaign tour to the West, but without the South his cause was hopeless.

Outside the South, the campaigns the two major parties waged stood out mostly for their placidity and their lack of enthusiasm. Both nominees had served in the White House, and neither inspired much warmth among party regulars. Cleveland's relations with Tammany Hall remained cool, indeed so cool that he urged campaign managers to push hard in Indiana, Illinois, and Wisconsin to offset the probable loss of New York. Cleveland's chances received a boost when Republican federal appeals judge Walter Q. Gresham, whose circuit comprised those three midwestern states, announced his support for the ex-president on the tariff issue. Some other Republican leaders simply sat on their hands. Blaine made only one campaign appearance, while Thomas Reed refused altogether to ride in what he called the Harrison "ice wagon."[23] The president, whose front-porch campaign had greatly enhanced his cause in 1888, could not repeat the effort because of the grave illness of his wife, who died two weeks before the election. Out of respect, Cleveland kept a low campaign profile, which he was inclined to do anyway.

On election day Cleveland won a commanding victory, defeating Harrison in the electoral college by 277 to 145, with Weaver taking 22 votes. Cleveland won all four northern doubtful states: New York, Indiana, Connecticut, and New Jersey. He also carried the normally Republican states of Illinois and Wisconsin, where the Democrats' appeals to labor and immigrants paid off. In the South, the Democrats' racial scare campaign turned back the Populist challenge; Cleveland won every former slave state. Harrison did, however, run reasonably well again in the Upper South, confirming the belief of many Republican leaders that the party should emphasize economic questions and leave civil rights issues alone. In most southern states, Weaver ran a distant third. The same was true in the Northeast and the Old Northwest, where in no state did he garner more than 5 percent of the popular vote. Weaver's message failed to appeal to workers in cities or to the farmers in the older agricultural regions of these states. The Populists did better in the trans-Mississippi farming and silver-producing regions, which were most in tune with the new party's money stance. In Kansas, Colorado, and Idaho, Populist fusion with the Democrats delivered those states to Weaver, while in Nevada, fusion with anti-Harrison Republicans won the state for the Populists. Weaver also got one electoral vote each from Oregon and North Dakota. His showing in California was good enough to throw the normally Republican state to Cleveland. Nationwide, Cleveland posted a margin of more than 360,000 over Harrison. Once again, however, he owed that edge to the lopsided southern results. Outside the South, Harrison surpassed Cleveland by nearly 450,000 votes.

In the congressional elections the Republicans managed to pick up thirty-nine more House seats than their dismal showing in 1890, but the Democrats would still have a commanding 60 percent majority. The Democrats also won control of the Senate, though by a much slimmer margin. Thus, for the first time since 1859, the Democrats would control the presidency, the House, and the Senate. That prospect unnerved the Republicans, who foresaw dire consequences for the nation's economy. "A little meddling with the tariff and currency," predicted one administration official, would "lead to widespread commercial distress before 1896."[24]

In his last annual message, Harrison valiantly but vainly sought to forestall such meddling. He offered an accounting of the nation's economic progress since 1860, citing increases in farm production, manufacturing, wages earned, number of employees, capital investments, savings banks deposits, and exports. R. G. Dun and Company's year-end economic assessment concurred, calling 1892 the "most prosperous year ever known in business." Harrison attributed much of this success to the beneficent effects of the protective tariff. But after the recent Democratic victory, he warned, the mere "threat of great tariff changes introduces so much uncertainty that an amount, not easily estimated, of business inaction and of diminished production will necessarily result." He set forth the prosperity at the close of his administration as a benchmark "from which to note the increase or decadence that new legislative policies may bring to us." He closed with a grave admonition: "Retrogression would be a crime."[25]

The Democrats paid little heed. Indeed, Cleveland and his allies relished the opportunity to undo what they regarded as years of Republican misgovernment. In his second inaugural address, on March 4, 1893, the new president invoked the precepts of classical liberalism, citing "laws governing our national health which we can no more evade than human life can escape the laws of God and nature." For good national health, he avowed, nothing was more vital than "a sound and stable currency." He depicted the recent election as a solemn referendum in which the "verdict of our voters . . . condemned the injustice of maintaining protection for protection's sake." Appealing to ancient Democratic Party doctrine, he insisted that "the only justification for taxing the people" was "the necessity for revenue." Protection begat paternalism, which in turn tempted the people to a "pitiful calculation of the sordid gain to be derived from their Government's maintenance." Instead, Cleveland said, "the lessons of paternalism ought to be unlearned and the better lesson taught that while the people should patriotically and cheerfully support their Government its functions do not include the support of the people."[26]

Within weeks Cleveland's notions about government came face-to-face with a severe challenge sparked by the Panic of 1893 and the ensuing deep depression. The recent rosy economic picture drawn by Harrison and financial analysts such as Dun had in part reflected the optimism inherent in a period of economic expansion. For years businessmen of all sorts—farmers, industrialists, railroad builders, town boomers—had gone into debt to expand their enterprises, gambling on the returns of a bright economic future. But in many sectors the expansion went beyond the demands of the market, leaving entrepreneurs with scant earnings to pay their burdensome debts. The first to suffer were farmers who had gone into debt to extend their landholdings or buy machinery. They succeeded wonderfully in expanding production, but their output soon outpaced the market, and prices collapsed. The ensuing agricultural breakdown had given rise to groups such as the Farmers' Alliance and the Populist Party, which saw inflation of the currency as the best means to rescue the desperate farmers.

A boom fueled by credit is inevitably vulnerable to shocks to business confidence. In late 1890 the collapse of Barings Bank in England had set American financial markets teetering, but a full-scale panic was averted when the New York Clearing House gave loans to exposed banks. New signs of trouble appeared after Cleveland's election. In November 1892 European investors who were worried about the stability of American currency increased their withdrawals of gold from the United States. Their redemption of government bonds threatened the Treasury's gold reserve that sustained the greenback circulation. Anxiety about the reserve further spurred investors and others to take greenbacks, silver coin, and silver certificates to the Treasury to exchange them for gold, causing the reserve to continue its downward slide toward $100 million, the level widely regarded as necessary to sustain the gold standard Turbulence also struck the stock markets of Wall Street, most notably a week before Cleveland's inauguration, when the collapse of the Philadelphia and Reading Railroad reverberated in a huge sell-off of shares. Seven weeks into the new administration, the Treasury gold reserve dipped below $100 million, completing the devastation of business confidence. Early May brought panic selling on Wall Street, and the economy quickly disintegrated. Credit dried up; railroads, banks, factories, mines, and other businesses closed; unemployment soared; and destitution stalked the cities as well as the countryside. As never before in their history, Americans looked to their government to devise a solution to their economic woes.

Cleveland had hoped to take his time after the election in leading the Democrats in fashioning a low-tariff replacement for the McKinley Act, but the panic altered his plans. He came under increasing pressure from distressed businessmen to shore up the government's finances by halting the purchase of silver under the

Sherman Silver Purchase Act of 1890. Cleveland himself became convinced of the absolute necessity of stopping the silver purchases as a way to ease the drain on the gold reserve and restore confidence. On June 30 he called a special session of Congress to convene in August to repeal the Sherman Act. In his message to the session, the president insisted that the nation's fundamental economic conditions were sound and favorable to prosperity. But, he said, "suddenly financial distrust and fear have sprung up on every side," a crippling anxiety "principally chargeable" to the operations of the Sherman Act. He urged Congress to act swiftly to repeal the law and thereby preserve the gold standard, restore business confidence, and put the nation on the road to recovery.[27]

Skeptics, some even within the administration, saw the nation's economic ills running more deeply than Cleveland supposed and doubted the effectiveness of silver repeal to achieve a real cure. Nonetheless, Cleveland was adamant and invoked every means at his disposal, including the lavish application of patronage, to persuade Democrats in Congress to meet his demand. Even so, he met resistance from many Democrats, including Nebraska congressman William Jennings Bryan, whose speech against repeal won him notice as a highly effective advocate of silver. The House passed the repeal measure fairly quickly, 239 to 108, but 78 Democrats voted against it. Moreover, before the final vote, the House considered (and rejected) several free coinage amendments that won substantial support among Democrats.

The sailing was even less smooth for Cleveland in the Senate. There he enlisted the aid of Finance Committee chairman Daniel Voorhees, a pro-silver inflationist from Indiana. To secure Voorhees's support, Cleveland gave him complete control of Hoosier patronage, leaving reformers such as Carl Schurz aghast at his apparent sacrifice of his civil service principles. But Voorhees's efforts for repeal could not prevent a prolonged filibuster by the measure's opponents. After nearly two months, worried Senate Democratic leaders fashioned a compromise that would leave the Sherman Act in operation for a year, permit the coinage of a small quantity of silver, and authorize the withdrawal of all greenbacks and Treasury notes of denominations under ten dollars. Although more than three-quarters of Senate Democrats signed on to the deal, an angry Cleveland refused. Under unrelenting administration pressure, the Senate finally passed the repeal bill on October 30, by a vote of 48 to 37. Cleveland got his way, but the 22-to-22 split among Democrats showed how deeply the president had driven a wedge between the silver and gold wings of his party.

Repeal gave a momentary boost to business confidence, but the feeling soon faded, and the economy continued its downward spiral into 1894. Business failures continued, and unemployment climbed to 20 percent. Nor did repeal shore up the Treasury's gold reserve. For the first time since 1866 the federal budget ran a deficit, and in January 1894 the administration was forced to make the first of four costly bond issues to replenish the government's finances. These loans proved highly advantageous to the creditors, and trafficking with rapacious banking interests became another black mark set against the increasingly unpopular Cleveland.

The economic crisis inflicted a devastating toll on Democrats' political fortunes. A week after Cleveland signed the repeal bill, the party lost heavily in a round of state elections. Historically Republican states such as Massachusetts, Pennsylvania, and Iowa reconfirmed their old faith by large majorities. In New York, Republicans carried the state ticket and the legislature handily. In Ohio, William McKinley scored a huge win in his bid for reelection as governor. McKinley had narrowly lost his House seat in the Democratic sweep of 1890, but he had rebounded the next year by winning the governorship. His victory by ten percentage points in 1893 fueled speculation about his presidential prospects in 1896.

Although Cleveland had asked the special session to focus on the silver issue, southern Democrats could not resist the opportunity that the party's majority status gave them to attack the legal vestiges of Reconstruction. Early in the session they presented a bill to repeal nearly forty sections of the Revised Statutes, originally passed in the Enforcement Acts of the early 1870s. The sections applied to federal election supervisors and deputy marshals and also established punishments for infractions of the right to vote. The Democrats insisted that these provisions violated both the Constitution and states' rights, while the Republicans warned that their repeal would leave the federal government helpless to defend blacks' right to vote in the South. Undeterred, the House Democrats pushed the measure through before the session ended. The Senate passed it during the regular session. Cleveland gave the bill his approval on February 12, 1894, the eighty-fifth anniversary of the birth of Abraham Lincoln. One Republican former senator bitterly predicted that the repeal would "leave the southern aristocracy again the masters of the country, as they were before their rebellion, until the people of the rest of the U.S. again wake up to the principles & practices of fair play."[28] For decades to come, southern Democrats would continue to wave their version of the bloodied gray shirt against the Republicans as the party of northern aggression and "negro domination." In the North, however, the bloody shirt was fading into history.

The main business of the regular session was the tariff. In late December, Ways and Means chairman William L. Wilson presented a bill that he estimated would reduce overall customs duties from the near 50 percent level of the McKinley Act to about 30 percent. The bill fulfilled Democrats' notions regarding lower duties on raw materials, which appealed to manufacturing interests in the Northeast, and it also expanded the free list. Southerners and consumers generally welcomed the reductions on manufactured goods. To compensate for lost revenue, the bill included a provision for a 2 percent tax on individual and corporate incomes of more than $4,000. At that high rate of exemption, this levy would have touched the

The Democrats are hopelessly at odds over the money question, and Grover Cleveland seems unwilling to do anything to bring them together. (Library of Congress)

earnings of fewer than 10 percent of American households. After a relatively short debate, the Wilson bill passed the House on February 1, 1894. It then headed for the Senate, where members of Cleveland's own party, as well as the Republicans, gave it intense scrutiny over the next several months.

While that scrutiny proceeded, congressional Democrats sought to heal some of the wounds left by silver repeal. They proposed a bill to coin the small amount of silver that had accumulated in the Treasury because of the difference between the purchase value and the face value of silver coins. This conciliatory gesture was neither inflationary nor a threat to the gold standard, and both houses passed it handily. Nonetheless, Cleveland considered it "ill advised and dangerous" and promptly vetoed it. The president thought his action made economic sense in trying to preserve what he considered the beneficial effects of the repeal measure, but politically, his veto proved disastrous. Prospects for reuniting the Democrats behind his leadership on any economic issue grew ever more remote, and Cleveland was fast becoming a pariah to many sections of his party. Within a week of his veto, the Democrats lost heavily in local elections in several states. This "political reaction," said *The New York Times*, was "due to hard times and popular discontent" which "the course of the Democrats for the last six months has tended to accelerate rather than retard."[29]

The spring and summer witnessed other explosions of discontent. From various parts of the country, so-called armies of the unemployed set off for Washington to petition for relief. The most famous of these groups was led by Ohio businessman Jacob Coxey, who advocated increased public works expenditures to put men to work. Cleveland had planted Secret Service agents in Coxey's army, and when it arrived at the Capitol on May 1, the police arrested Coxey for trespassing and dispersed his band of followers.

Discontent also burst forth in labor unrest, with hundreds of thousands of workers going on strike to protest wage cuts and layoffs.

In late spring, a strike by workers at the Pullman Palace Car Company near Chicago soon evolved into a widespread sympathy strike conducted by the American Railway Union against most of the nation's major railroads. At the urging of rail companies, the administration went to court and secured a sweeping injunction against the strikers. Cleveland also ordered out federal troops, ostensibly to protect the transport of the U.S. mails, but in effect to break the strike. With the arrival of troops, the strike was soon brought to a violent end. Although propertied and middle-class Americans hailed Cleveland for saving civilization, the alienation of vast numbers of workers from the Democrats was complete.

On the same day that Cleveland ordered troops to Chicago, the Senate passed its version of the Wilson tariff bill. The upper House, where the Democrats held a narrow majority, had amended the bill 634 times. The revised bill restored duties on more than forty items, including sugar, iron ore, and coal, that the Wilson bill had assigned to the free list, and it raised other customs duties to an average eight percentage points above the Wilson level. Lobbyists had exerted intense pressure, and senators, including Democrats led by Maryland's Arthur P. Gorman, worked to retain protective rates on items produced in their home states. Having squandered his leverage on the silver fight, Cleveland could do little to salvage the Wilson reforms. When negotiations on the bill in a House-Senate conference committee bogged down, Cleveland authorized Wilson to release a letter from him accusing the recalcitrant Democrats of "party perfidy and party dishonor."[30] This obnoxious attempt to shame his party opponents into compliance made them dig in their heels all the more deeply. The Senate refused to back down, and the House finally accepted the Senate's version. An adamant Cleveland withheld his approval, and in late August the Wilson-Gorman Tariff became law without his signature.

Shortly thereafter, Congress adjourned, and Democrats headed home to face constituents grown hostile over what they saw as the party's bumbling incapacity to deal with the nation's economic crisis. With midterm congressional elections little more than two months away, Democrats were hard-pressed to defend the conduct of either Congress or the administration. The assertion by the 1894 Democratic campaign book that the crisis that had struck early in Cleveland's term was "the direct result of the preceding four years of Republican rule" convinced few voters. Much more persuasive were the arguments by Benjamin Harrison, William McKinley, Thomas Reed, and other Republicans that the Democrats' narrow conceptions of government were utterly inadequate either to meet the crisis at hand or to manage a modern industrializing society. "Why is it that amid all the resources of the land we are suffering?" McKinley asked one campaign audience. "I can answer in a word. The Democrats are running the Government, and nothing else is running."[31]

The outcome of the November elections demonstrated that most of the electorate accepted that analysis. In an unprecedented shift of congressional strength, Republicans regained control of the House by a two-to-one majority. In the tier of states that stretched from Iowa and Minnesota across the old Free State section of the country to Maine, Republicans elected 186 congressmen and the Democrats 9. West of that section, Republicans won every seat except three that went to Populists. The GOP even managed to crack the Solid South, winning 38 of 127 seats in the old slave states. The Republicans also gained control of the Senate.

It was an election that ended many political careers and helped to launch others. In Nebraska, two-term Democratic congressman William Jennings Bryan decided not to run for reelection, but to set his sights on the U.S. Senate; the Democrats' loss of the state legislature killed that dream. Among the biggest winners was a Republican who did not receive a single vote. Ohio governor William McKinley was not on the ballot, but he took an extensive campaign trip, making more than three hundred speeches in one-third of the states, including many in Bryan's Nebraska. McKinley's carefully orchestrated tour boosted him into the front rank of possible Republican presidential nominees in 1896, and in his own way, the young but ambitious Bryan inched his way toward a similar goal on the Democratic side.

SIX

The Emerging Republican Majority

In the early 1890s the equilibrium that had characterized American politics for nearly two decades had given way to a period of tremendous flux. In 1890 and 1892, triumphant Democrats entertained hopes that they were at last becoming the nation's dominant and sustained majority party, but the disastrous second Cleveland administration brought those hopes to ruin in 1894. Now it was the Republicans' turn to try to retain the allegiance of the masses of voters who had swung their way. Clearly, economic issues now stood uppermost on the GOP agenda and in voters' minds, and with each passing day, signs pointed toward the party's nomination of William McKinley for president in 1896.

Long an admirer of James G. Blaine, McKinley had first entered Congress in 1877 and soon made the tariff his legislative specialty. As chairman of the resolutions committee at the Republican conventions of 1884 and 1888, he oversaw the drawing of planks that committed the party to high protectionism. As chairman of the House Ways and Means Committee in the Fifty-first Congress, he took the lead in putting that theory into law. Even before Blaine's death, in early 1893, McKinley had emerged as the Republican Party's chief spokesman on the tariff issue. And in 1894 and 1895 he proved a worthy successor to Blaine in his willingness to travel around the country to speak on behalf of fellow Republicans. Like Blaine, he amassed an abundance of political IOUs.

In the quest for national convention delegates in 1896, McKinley's campaign benefited from the able leadership of Ohio industrialist Mark Hanna, who had dabbled in politics for years. Although some contemporaries and later historians portrayed McKinley as a puppet or creature of the wealthy Hanna, McKinley was the directing partner in their relationship. As the convention approached, the tide was with McKinley, but his nomination did not go unchallenged. Most notably, some Republicans preferred Thomas B. Reed, who had distinguished himself as a fearsome debater in the House and a powerful Speaker in the Fifty-first and Fifty-fourth Congresses. Yet Reed's forcefulness went hand in hand with a sarcastic treatment of adversaries that many found off-putting. He had little love for McKinley, and as for his own chances for the nomination, Reed said, Republicans "might do worse, and they probably will."[1]

Worse or not, McKinley had the nomination fairly sewn up by the late spring. At the national convention in mid-June, the Ohioan garnered nearly 75 percent of the delegate votes on the sole ballot. The platform clearly fit the nominee. It exalted protectionism and denounced the Democrats' Wilson-Gorman Tariff for nullifying the Harrison administration's reciprocity agreements: "Protection builds up domestic industry and trade and secures our own market for ourselves; reciprocity builds up foreign trade and finds an outlet for our surplus." The platform gave only perfunctory mention to civil rights, demanding (in the passive voice) that every citizen "shall be allowed to cast one free and unrestricted ballot, and that such ballot shall be counted."

The most controversial plank dealt with the currency. McKinley, who had exhibited silver leanings early in his congressional career, had recently said little on the subject, but now he sanctioned a strong statement portraying the party as "unreservedly for sound money." Republicans, said the currency plank, "are therefore opposed to the free coinage of silver, except by international agreement with the leading commercial nations of the earth, which agreement we pledge ourselves to promote; and until such agreement can be obtained, the existing gold standard must be maintained."[2] This was too much for a small group of silver supporters who proposed an alternative plank for free coinage of silver at sixteen to one with gold. The delegates rejected the substitute overwhelmingly, and twenty-three silver delegates (out of a total exceeding nine hundred) withdrew from the convention. The Populists hoped to secure their support, but all eyes turned next to Chicago, where the Democratic convention would soon confront the vexatious question.

The hostility that large numbers of Democrats felt for Grover Cleveland, their own party's president, was on full display in Chicago. The resolutions committee submitted a platform that, without citing Cleveland by name, condemned "trafficking with banking syndicates," objected to "government by injunction as a new and highly dangerous form of oppression," and declared that "no man should be eligible for a third term of the Presidential office." When a minority of the committee proposed an amendment to "commend the honesty, economy, courage, and fidelity" of the Cleveland administration, Senator Benjamin Tillman of South Carolina offered a counteramendment to "denounce the administration of President Cleveland as undemocratic and tyran[n]ical." The convention rejected the commendatory amendment by a vote of 357 in favor to 564 against, after which Tillman withdrew his motion as having been essentially endorsed by the previous vote. In effect, five-eighths of the delegates voted to declare Cleveland anathema.[3]

The platform's money plank also represented a rejection of the president's policies. It demanded "the free and unlimited coinage of both silver and gold at the present legal ratio of 16 to 1 without waiting for the aid or consent of any other nation." The minority of the resolutions committee countered with a plank declaring that free coinage of silver would "inflict irreparable evils" on the economy and favoring the "rigid maintenance" of the gold standard until the securing of an international agreement for silver coinage. The dueling planks sparked a heated floor debate that climaxed with a speech by William Jennings Bryan, who advocated passionately for silver and, not coincidentally, drew the delegates' attention to himself. Speaking, he said, for "all the toiling masses," Bryan closed with a solemn notice to the enemies of silver: "You shall not press down upon the brow of labor this crown of thorns. You shall not crucify mankind upon a cross of gold." The delegates erupted into a delirious demonstration for the speech and for the cause. The convention rejected the minority plank by a vote of 303 to 626, thus committing the party to free coinage of silver. The platform also called for a revenue tariff but opposed any "agitation" for a change in customs legislation "until the money question is settled."[4]

The money plank made clear that no eastern gold-standard Democrat had a ghost of a chance for the party's presidential nomination. As one speaker put it, the convention needed simply "to name the candidate who will fit the platform."[5] The contest boiled down to one between sixty-year-old former congressman Richard "Silver Dick" Bland, who had been at the forefront of the silver crusade for decades, and Bryan, who at thirty-six was about half Bland's age and had at least twice his vigor to push the crusade forward. Bland led the first three ballots, with Bryan closing in at second place. On the fourth ballot the Nebraskan moved ahead, spurring a rush, and on the fifth ballot Bryan won the nomination. To run with Bryan, the convention nominated Arthur Sewall, a wealthy Maine businessman and banker who backed silver.

Not all Democrats joined the celebration of Bryan's nomination. During the balloting, about a quarter of the delegates boycotted the voting or voted for a token gold candidate from Pennsylvania. Back in Washington, a "dazed" Cleveland dismissed the convention outcome as "an ill wind that blows no good to anyone," and he denied

all responsibility for "the disasters that await the Democratic party."
Two months later Gold Democrats gathered in Indianapolis to nominate an alternative candidate, Senator John Palmer of Illinois, on a
platform that praised Cleveland, condemned the Chicago platform,
and upheld the gold standard. Palmer had no chance, but the increasingly isolated Cleveland "thank[ed] God that the glorious principles of our party have found defenders who will not permit them
to be polluted by impure hands."[6]

More important than Palmer's nomination for the course of the
campaign was the role the Populists played. People's Party leaders
had expected to pick up silverite defectors once the two major parties had committed to gold, but the Democrats' embrace of silver
upset that plan. A struggle arose between so-called middle-of-the-
road Populists, who thought the party should nominate its own candidate on the broad Populist reform platform—even at the risk of
defeat—and fusionists, who favored nominating Bryan with his silver emphasis, even at the risk of submerging the People's Party's
independent identity. At the St. Louis convention, the latter group
prevailed, although the Populists would not accept the easterner
Sewall for vice president and nominated the radical Thomas Watson
of Georgia instead. The platform echoed the Democrats' call for free
coinage, but it also included such Populist reform demands as government ownership of the railroads and public works spending to put
idle labor to work. The division over the vice presidency led to fusion
in some areas and confusion in others, as party leaders in the individual states fielded an array of electoral tickets in diverse configu-
rations. Bryan stood by Sewall, paid little attention to the Populists,
and waged his campaign as a Democrat.

In that campaign, however, Bryan encountered some trouble in
trying to enlist fellow Democrats in his fight. Wealthy men in the
party refused to make their customary contributions to the nominee's war chest, and in the anti-silver Northeast, party cadres remained unenthusiastic. Almost half of the party's newspapers,

William Jennings Bryan, with multiple presidential nominations, has trouble establishing a secure, cohesive base for his campaign. (Library of Congress)

including some large metropolitan dailies, withheld their support or came out for McKinley. It was thus left to Bryan to spearhead his own campaign, and he rose to the occasion magnificently. Although a few previous nominees, most notably Blaine in 1884, had taken speaking tours, Bryan in a sense invented the modern nonstop traveling presidential campaign. During much of his relentless journey he often traveled with only a few associates, making his own arrangements and lugging his own bags. He logged 18,000 miles traveling through 27 states and making 600 speeches, nearly always focused on the silver issue. Crowds were usually large and, outside the Northeast, often enthusiastic. If nothing else, people saw a visit and a speech from Bryan as a curiosity, and his trip garnered ample free publicity for the cash-strapped campaign.

Yet to some degree Bryan's tour played into the hands of Republicans who sought to portray the Democratic/Populist nominee as a dangerous demagogue bent on inciting class warfare. John Hay (who later became McKinley's secretary of state) described Bryan as a "half-baked glib little briefless jack-leg lawyer, running around the country . . . denouncing capital and . . . promising the millennium to everybody with a hole in his 'pants,' and destruction to everybody with a clean shirt." In contrast, Republicans portrayed McKinley as the embodiment of solidity, good sense, and dependability, whose embrace of a stable currency, tariff protectionism, and reciprocity made him the "Advance Agent of Prosperity." McKinley himself stayed at home in Canton and, taking his cue from Benjamin Harrison in 1888, conducted a highly effective front-porch campaign. He not only addressed three-quarters of a million listeners from thirty states, but his more than three hundred speeches appeared in newspapers across the nation. With an overflowing campaign treasury (at $3.5 million, about seven times Bryan's funds), the Republicans dispatched hundreds of surrogate speakers around the country. They prepared 275 different, carefully targeted tracts and distributed about 220 million copies, or more than a dozen pamphlets for each American voter.[7]

McKinley's approach to the South demonstrated how far the Republicans had moved away from "bloody shirt" or Force bill notions. Emphasizing a burgeoning sense of national unity, he insisted that "the feeling of distrust and hostility between the sections is everywhere vanishing." Again echoing Harrison, he urged southerners to join the drive toward prosperity that Republican policies would produce. Moreover, McKinley and the Republicans refused to follow Bryan in focusing solely on the money question. They urged Americans to consider what the Wilson-Gorman Tariff had wrought and the vital need to revive the protective principle. "Will the people," McKinley asked, "turn to that party for relief whose policy has created the conditions under which they are suffering and from which they are crying out to be relieved?" Bryan, McKinley declared, was "advocating all the policies of the Democratic Party which have been injurious to the American people [a low tariff], and rejecting all that are good [a sound currency]." "The people want neither free trade nor free silver," McKinley insisted. "The one will degrade our labor, the other our money."[8]

On election day McKinley won a smashing victory, posting a popular vote margin over Bryan of more than 600,000, the largest since Ulysses S. Grant's reelection in 1872. The electoral vote stood at 271 to 176. McKinley completely swept the North, taking every state from Maine in the Northeast westward all the way to Minnesota, Iowa, and North Dakota. He also made inroads into the South, capturing the Border States of Delaware, Maryland, and West Virginia by comfortable margins, and Kentucky very narrowly. His sectional conciliationist posture also allowed him to make respectable runs in the Upper South states of Virginia, Tennessee, and North Carolina, in all of which he garnered more than 45 percent. In the Deep South, however, disfranchisement of blacks had taken its toll. In most of these states, less than 30 percent of the vote was counted for McKinley; in Mississippi it was 6.9 percent. Conversely, the South gave Bryan three-fourths of his electoral-vote total. The other major areas of support for the Democratic/Populist nominee were the western Plains states and the new silver-producing states of the Rocky Mountain West.

The Republicans won 57 percent of the seats in the House of Representatives and would hold 53 percent in the Senate. Although the Populists could claim their largest representation ever in the Fifty-fifth Congress (more than twenty in the House), the Populist Bryan-Watson ticket had won only 2 percent of the presidential vote. The People's Party ceased to be a factor in American politics.

After the election, the Bryan camp complained that employers had bullied workers into voting for McKinley with threats of plant closings and other dire consequences should Bryan win. The impact of such tactics, if they did occur, paled next to the benefit that Bryan, like previous Democratic candidates, derived from widespread disfranchisement of blacks in the South. In six states of the Deep South, voter participation averaged 34.9 percent, less than half the national rate of 79.3 percent. Bryan lost not because of intimidation of voters, but because he failed to convince a sufficient number of Americans that inflation of the money supply through free coinage of silver would benefit them. Some farmers and others in debt saw hope in his offering, but creditors obviously did not, and creditors included a larger slice of the populace than just rich bankers. Anyone on a fixed income or who had money deposited in a bank or owned a bond had reason to fear a diminution in the value of the currency. So too did laborers who instinctively believed that inflation would increase the prices they had to pay far faster than it would the wages they received. McKinley had succeeded in convincing enough voters that a program of tariff protection and trade expansion through reciprocity, coupled with a possibility of "safe" currency expansion through international bimetallism, offered the key to a revival of prosperity.

McKinley regarded the election outcome as a ringing endorsement of these policies and of the Republicans' general notions of

William McKinley takes the oath of office as president while a dejected Grover Cleveland relinquishes his official cares. (Library of Congress)

activist government. In his inaugural address on March 4, 1897, he insisted that "the restoration of confidence and the revival of business, which men of all parties so much desire, depend more largely upon the prompt, energetic, and intelligent action of Congress than upon any other single agency affecting the situation." Specifically on the tariff issue, he said, "The people have declared that such legislation should be had as will give ample protection and encouragement to the industries and the development of our country." But he also called for "the re-enactment and extension of the reciprocity principle of the law of 1890." Regarding the money question, he promised to push for an international agreement on coinage, but in the interim, he asserted, "the commanding verdict of the people" was that the gold standard should be upheld.[9]

On the southern question, McKinley gave no indication that the Republicans would use their return to power to redress the injustice in the region as they had tried to do during the Fifty-first Congress. Indeed, he declared that "free and fair elections" were "more universally enjoyed to-day than ever before." McKinley's administration marked the effective abandonment of blacks' rights by the GOP. The president gave precedence to his claim that "the North and the South no longer divide on the old lines," and he promised that he would "do nothing, and permit nothing to be done, that will arrest or disturb this growing sentiment of unity and co-operation." This approach showed clearly in the fall of 1898, when, in the aftermath of an election in Wilmington, North Carolina, savage racial violence left at least fourteen blacks dead. The administration monitored the incident but took no substantive action. Five weeks later, on a tour through the South, the president assured whites of the "cordial feeling now happily existing between the North and South." He urged blacks to look for improvement through self-help and industrial training, in the spirit of Booker T. Washington's Atlanta Compromise. "Nothing in the world commands more respect than skill and industry," he told one black audience. "Keep on. You will solve your own problem." Leaving blacks essentially to their own devices,

McKinley gave a much higher priority to sectional reconciliation. Although a handful of die-hard civil rights advocates complained, McKinley had at last retired the "bloody shirt" and eliminated blacks' grievances and the southern question from the national agenda.[10]

The president emphasized sectional harmony in part to project national unity in an increasingly dangerous world. In discussing foreign affairs in his inaugural address, he proposed to "cultivate relations of peace and amity with all the nations of the world," and he invoked the nation's long-standing and wise "policy of non-interference with the affairs of foreign governments." As European nations were sharpening their imperial knives, he avowed, "We want no wars of conquest; we must avoid the temptation of territorial aggression. War should never be entered upon until every agency of peace has failed; peace is preferable to war in almost every contingency."[11] On taking office, the new president made no specific mention of the situation in Cuba, where the colonial government had been engaged since 1895 in a brutal struggle to suppress a popular uprising against Spanish rule. Yet events in Cuba would soon put McKinley's commitment to peace to a severe test and open the way for a fundamental transformation in the nation's relations abroad.

On the domestic front, the Republicans moved swiftly to deal with the tariff, which they regarded as the most pressing issue. After nearly thirty years of surpluses, the federal government had run a deficit since 1893. In his inaugural, McKinley called a special session of Congress to meet eleven days later, sooner than Abraham Lincoln had convened Congress during the secession crisis. McKinley urged the legislature to pass a new tariff law that would not only provide sufficient revenue to rectify the fiscal problem but would also afford protection to American producers and expand trade. After speedy passage of a bill in the House, the Senate, where the Republican margin was slimmer, deliberated into the summer and came under tremendous pressure from economic interests desiring protection. The resulting Dingley Tariff, approved in late July, raised rates to an overall average of 57 percent, a peacetime record and higher than McKinley had planned. Receipts rose steadily, although the government did not run a surplus until fiscal year 1900, in considerable part because of costs associated with the Spanish-American War.

Increasingly, McKinley had embraced the idea of reciprocity, and he was pleased that the new law revived the program, albeit according to a formula more complicated than that outlined in the 1890 tariff law. The president appointed the seasoned trade diplomat John A. Kasson as a special envoy to conduct negotiations under the terms of the Dingley Act. Kasson completed four minor executive agreements, which had a relatively small impact on trade, but thirteen treaties that would have lowered trade barriers significantly never emerged from the Senate. Thus the administration accomplished little under the Dingley reciprocity regime, but it did carry the principle of reciprocity forward into the twentieth century, when it bore more fruit.

Following through on another campaign promise, McKinley appointed Colorado senator Edward Wolcott to head a commission to pursue an international agreement regarding silver coinage. Wolcott spent several months in Europe in 1897, trying to persuade France and Great Britain to endorse the idea. Neither was terribly enthusiastic, and when the British signaled their final refusal in October, Wolcott's mission collapsed. Some silver supporters accused McKinley of insincerity or halfheartedness on behalf of international bimetallism, but other circumstances sealed the doom of the silver movement. A decline in the price of silver undercut arguments that the white metal could be a reliable part of a stable national currency. Even more important, a rebound in the nation's economy weakened the case for silver inflation. Crop failures in Europe and elsewhere opened up a vast market for agricultural commodities, and huge crop yields put money in American farmers' pockets. Industrial production also moved into higher gear, again to meet a burgeoning foreign demand. Increased exports brought gold back into the country, and increased gold production in the United States, Canada, and South Africa further multiplied gold stocks. The Treasury's gold reserve climbed to $137 million by the end of 1897 and to $245 million by the middle of 1898. Returning prosperity did much to establish the gold standard in practice, and the Republicans embodied the principle in law with the Gold Standard Act of 1900, thus bringing to a close the currency battle that had roiled the politics of the 1890s.

State and local elections in a handful of states in 1897 proved to be inconclusive for gauging public reaction to the McKinley administration's first year. For reasons that varied from state to state, Republicans saw their strength generally decline from levels achieved during the presidential year, and they lost the key state of New York. In Ohio, the incumbent Republican governor won reelection with 50.3 percent of the vote in a field of eight candidates, and Mark Hanna won election to the Senate by a razor-thin margin in the legislature. McKinley himself, however, enjoyed wide popularity. In Nebraska, where a fusion ticket defeated the Republicans, the Populists felt compelled to insist that citizens should be "thankful to Providence rather than to any man for the measure of prosperity with which our state has been blessed."[12] McKinley had carefully cultivated excellent relations with the press, which paid off in favorable coverage. Moreover, he rejected the reclusiveness of the beleaguered Grover Cleveland, and he traveled widely and spoke often, carrying his message of hope and economic renewal directly to the people. In this he followed a pattern set by Benjamin Harrison, whom he had observed from his seat in the Fifty-first Congress. With a much warmer personality than Harrison's, McKinley proved more successful at forging bonds with party leaders around the country.

While McKinley and other Republicans moved to take credit for a reviving economy, foreign affairs entered into political discourse to a degree unseen for decades. Attention focused on Cuba. Americans grew increasingly disturbed by the harsh tactics Spain had adopted to quell the revolution among the island's people. In order to isolate rebels, Spanish authorities forced the rural population into garrison towns or concentration camps, where lack of food and water and wretched conditions led to hundreds of thousands of deaths. In addition, the violence threatened to destroy American-owned plantations and other investment property, and the ongoing struggle disrupted commercial relations with the island. Both sides committed atrocities, but Cuban juntas in America and American newspapers especially dramatized Spanish outrages. During the election campaign of 1897, Ohio Republicans extended their "sympathy to the patriots of Cuba" and expressed confidence in McKinley's ability to handle the situation "in accordance with wise statesmanship and a vigorous foreign policy." Buckeye Democrats went further, demanding "immediate recognition of the belligerent rights of the republic of Cuba."[13]

McKinley chose to move more slowly, deliberately pursuing a series of diplomatic steps designed to persuade Spain to curtail its brutality and accept American mediation. But the president had no desire to impose a solution unacceptable to the Cubans; and their ambition for nothing short of independence, coupled with Spain's refusal to grant it peacefully, put events on course to an inevitable American intervention. In October 1897 Spain announced an end to the "reconcentration" policy and promised a plan for internal autonomy for Cuba, but evidence soon surfaced that cast doubt on Spain's commitment to these changes. In mid-January 1898 Spanish loyalists (plus Spanish soldiers) rioted in Havana against autonomy. On February 9 the sensationalist *New York Journal* published an intercepted letter in which the Spanish minister to the United States criticized McKinley as a weak and vain politician and indicated Spain's insincerity regarding reform. A week later an American warship, the *Maine*, which McKinley had dispatched to observe developments, exploded in Havana harbor, resulting in 266 deaths. A naval court of inquiry cited an external cause, such as a mine, and Americans were quick to blame Spain, either for destroying the ship or for lacking sufficient control in Cuban waters to prevent its destruction.

Shortly after the naval report, McKinley sent an ultimatum to Madrid, demanding that Spain truly end reconcentration, grant an armistice in Cuba, and negotiate with the insurgents in good faith through American mediation. If the combatants could not reach a solution by October 1, McKinley would assume the role of arbiter and settle the matter. After Spain again rejected mediation and refused an armistice until the rebels asked for it, McKinley at last began to prepare a war message to Congress. Although Spain relented to a degree and offered to cease fighting, it still refused American mediation, and McKinley proceeded with his message. By the end of April the United States was at war with Spain. Some critics of McKinley accused him of caving in to pro-war pressure from the press and Congress, but in fact, in the spirit of his war-as-a-last-resort comment in his inaugural address, he had tried to achieve his aims peacefully. He moved forthrightly toward war to achieve them when negotiation failed. Disavowing any ulterior imperialist motive, Congress attached to the war resolution a proviso called the Teller Amendment, which renounced any intention to annex Cuba.

John Hay famously described the conflict as "a splendid little war," but he and others fully understood its pivotal character.[14] Actual fighting lasted little more than a hundred days, but it was far-flung. Americans easily defeated the Spanish not only in Cuba and neighboring Puerto Rico, but halfway around the globe in their island colonies of Guam and the Philippines as well. In an armistice arranged in McKinley's office on August 12, Spain agreed to leave Cuba, ceded Guam and Puerto Rico to the United States, and consented to a peace conference to settle the fate of the Philippines. (In

July the United States had annexed the independent country of Hawaii, a move that Harrison had proposed but Cleveland had blocked.) McKinley appointed a five-person commission to the Paris Peace Conference that began October 1. With an eye to the ratification struggle ahead, the president included three senators on the commission, including the Delaware Democrat George Gray. As never before, the United States had taken a place on the world stage.

The midterm congressional elections of 1898 proceeded in the afterglow of the administration's military victory and the prospect of fruitful negotiations in Paris. McKinley himself plunged into the campaign, taking an extended speaking tour through the midwest as Harrison had done in 1890. The trip was ostensibly nonpolitical, but McKinley touched on themes that he hoped would help solidify and perpetuate the Republican majority that had emerged in the elections of 1894 and 1896. He celebrated the new prosperity, noting that the country had rebounded from "industrial depression to industrial activity," from "labor seeking employment to employment seeking labor." The United States, he declared, had "accepted war for humanity," and one of its most important results was to make the North and South, "united in holy alliance," determined "to stand by the government of the United States." As the negotiations proceeded in Paris, McKinley worked to prepare Americans to accept new acquisitions. "We cannot shirk the obligations of the victory," he said. "Territory sometimes comes to us when we go to war in a holy cause." But more was involved than righteous duty. "We have pretty much everything in this country to make it happy," he told an audience in Iowa, "but we want new markets, and as trade follows the flag, it looks very much as if we were going to have new markets."[15]

Most Republicans gladly followed their robust new leader in war and peace. In New York they nominated a well-known hero of the war, Theodore Roosevelt, for governor, and expressed confidence that McKinley would conclude a treaty that would "satisfy the conscience, the judgment, and the high purpose of the American people." Democrats were hard-pressed to run against the patriotic nationalism embraced by McKinley and his party. Many focused their criticism on Secretary Russell Alger's mismanagement of the War Department and the consequent suffering of American soldiers in the field. But the Democratic platform in New York exemplified the party's awkward position regarding the war itself: "We rejoice that the Democracy has been connected with every honorable and creditable step in the war, and with nothing that is dishonorable or discreditable." Within each party, some entertained doubts about the wisdom of imperial acquisitions. Bryan, who had become a colonel in a Nebraska volunteer regiment, warned that "if a contest undertaken for the sake of humanity degenerates into a war of conquest, we shall find it difficult to meet the charge of having added hypocrisy to greed." Former president Benjamin Harrison declined to campaign for fellow Republicans, finding himself not "in sympathy with the extreme expansion views that are being advocated."[16]

Nonetheless, Republicans could congratulate themselves that they fared well in the midterm elections, during which a president's party often suffers losses in Congress. In the House of Representatives, the Democrats gained fifty seats, largely at the expense of the Populists, but the GOP lost only nineteen and held on to a comfortable majority. In the Senate, the Republicans expanded their majority by six seats and would occupy fifty-three of the ninety seats in the Fifty-sixth Congress. GOP candidates also did well in state elections in several key northern states. Thus Republicans held on to their new status as the nation's majority party, and they had ample reason for optimism for McKinley's reelection in 1900. "You have pulled us through with your own strength," Hay assured the president; "this makes the work for 1900 simple and easy."[17]

Yet McKinley still confronted the task of winning approval of the treaty with Spain under negotiation in Paris. Since the point early in the war when the American navy had sunk the Spanish fleet at Manila, McKinley had been drifting toward the conclusion that the

United States should retain control of the Philippine Islands, and ten days before the election he had instructed the American peace commissioners to that effect. In the treaty signed at Paris on December 10, 1898, Spain ceded the Philippines, Guam, and Puerto Rico to the United States and relinquished control of Cuba, while the United States agreed to pay Spain $20 million. The momentous step outlined in the treaty occasioned a passionate debate in the Senate and in the country between those who welcomed the acquisitions as strategically and economically beneficial and those who believed that this "imperial" drive violated America's fundamental values. In the Senate, Republicans constituted far less than the two-thirds necessary to ratify the treaty, and McKinley could not even count on all the GOP senators. In late December he took a trip through the South, reiterating his encomiums to sectional harmony in part to win Dixie senators for the treaty, and he was not above dispensing patronage favors to procure their support. Just a few days before the scheduled vote, open fighting erupted in the Philippines between American military forces and native insurgents resisting American control, thereby confirming some senators in their sense of America's responsibility in the islands and others in their sense of the injustice the United States was committing. After a prolonged struggle, on February 6, 1899, the Senate ratified the treaty by a vote of 57 to 27, just one vote more than necessary.

The debate over imperialism did not cease with the treaty ratification, especially since the war against the Philippine insurgents dragged on, costing many more lives than the war with Spain. The Anti-Imperialist League, whose leaders included such prominent figures as Grover Cleveland, John Sherman, and Carl Schurz, denounced annexation of the islands as "inconsistent with the principles of this Republic, and fraught with danger to its peace and to the peace of the world."[18]

Bryan was a leading voice against imperialism, and he and other Democrats saw the question as a powerful weapon against the

Republicans. In several states in the state election campaign in 1899, the Democrats not only endorsed free silver and Bryan's re-nomination but also condemned, as the Ohio party put it, the "un-lawful" use of American soldiers "to crush and destroy dawning republicanism in the Orient." Republicans, in contrast, celebrated the nation's prosperity and the liberation of Cuba and more temper-ately stood by the administration's efforts in the Philippines.[19]

Both Bryan and McKinley hit the campaign trail that fall. At Fremont, in the president's home state, Bryan charged that the Re-publican Party proposed "to buy the Filipinos at $2 a head and kill them, because they claim to own them by right of purchase from a decayed monarchy." McKinley once again took an extended tour through nine midwestern states, winding up in Ohio, where he in-sisted that territories acquired by the recent treaty were "ours just as much as any part of the great public domain," and that the Amer-ican flag flew over them not as a "flag of tyranny," but as a symbol of "justice and liberty and right and civilization." Rejoicing in the nation's prosperity, he told an audience in the industrial city of Youngstown that he found nothing "more encouraging or more help-ful to me than the cheer given by the men as they came out of the mills and waved their shining dinner-buckets, now full when once they were empty." The Republicans carried Ohio and several other states handily, while in Nebraska victory by a fusion ticket sup-ported by Bryan helped keep his presidential prospects alive.[20]

As expected, the campaign of 1899 proved to be a prelude to the presidential contest in 1900. Republicans enthusiastically renomi-nated the president, echoing his speech in Youngstown by adopting the slogan "Four more years of the full dinner pail." The closest thing to drama at the party's national convention was the selection of a vice presidential nominee. McKinley left the decision to the dele-gates, who chose the forty-one-year-old governor of New York, Theo-dore Roosevelt. The platform boasted that Republicans had kept their two main promises from 1896—to enact a protective tariff and a law establishing the gold standard—and that "prosperity more

The Republican ticket for 1900: William McKinley, clearly aged by four years in the White House, and the robust Theodore Roosevelt (Library of Congress)

general and more abundant than we have ever known has followed these enactments." On the civil rights question, now virtually invisible in national politics, the platform said simply that the statutory and constitutional devices southern states had adopted to bar African Americans from voting "should be condemned." The Republicans pronounced the war against Spain "a war for liberty and human rights" and justified the ongoing struggle against the Philippine insurgents as "the high duty of the Government to maintain its authority, to put down armed insurrection and to confer the blessings of liberty and civilization upon all the rescued peoples."[21]

Bryan won renomination as easily as McKinley did. The Nebraskan still enjoyed immense popularity among Democrats, although some, mostly from the Northeast, were simply resigned to his nomination in a year when they considered the party likely to lose. For vice president the Democrats chose Adlai E. Stevenson, a defender of silver who had held the office in Cleveland's second term. This gesture toward unity could not entirely mask the continued factionalism among Democrats. Easterners who considered the money question settled hoped to focus the campaign on the imperialism issue, but Bryan was determined to give equal play to silver. The convention's platform represented a compromise of sorts in that it cited the "burning issue of imperialism" as "the paramount issue of the campaign" but also called for the free and unlimited coinage of silver. In reaction to a business merger wave that had swept over the country since 1895, the platform included a lengthy passage that pledged "unceasing warfare" against "private monopoly" and denounced Republicans for fostering and protecting trusts "in return for campaign subscriptions and political support." The Republicans had also condemned "all conspiracies and combinations intended to restrict business," but Democrats claimed that they had failed to use their power to "curtail the absorbing power" that the trusts wielded.[22]

As a sitting president, McKinley kept a low profile during the campaign. In his absence from the stump, Roosevelt and Republican national chairman Mark Hanna emerged as the campaign's leading speakers. Yet McKinley made an important contribution in setting forth his ideas in his letter of acceptance. He called upon Americans to reject Bryan's silver panacea as emphatically as they had done in 1896. He took pride that protection and reciprocity had been "the first pledges of Republican victory" to be enacted by his administration. He hailed the return of prosperity and the burgeoning of exports, and he called for "prohibitory and penal legislation" against the trusts. McKinley devoted about half of the letter to a detailed explanation of his Philippine policy. His aim, he insisted, was to "bring the benefits of liberty and good government to these wards of the nation . . . not for exploitation, but for humanity."[23] As the campaign was getting under way, the administration enhanced its foreign policy sheen when Secretary of State John Hay issued his second Open Door note, solemnly warning Western powers to respect China's territorial integrity in their efforts to quell anti-Western violence in the so-called Boxer Rebellion.

Bryan's campaign was as poorly funded as his effort four years previously, and once again he bore the brunt of the speaking. It was an uphill fight, and he was unable to gain much traction against the well-organized, well-financed Republicans. Silver had lost its luster, and Bryan's early attempt to harry McKinley on the imperialism issue sputtered after the president's letter of acceptance. Bryan switched the argument to the trusts, but Republicans countered that Democrats were involved in some of the big consolidations and had done little to combat them when Cleveland was in power. The simple fact was that in the midst of general prosperity, Bryan could say or do little to counteract the Republicans' promise of "four more years of the full dinner-pail."

The outcome was never in doubt. McKinley swamped Bryan by more than 850,000 votes, the largest margin of victory in American history up to that time. The electoral vote count was 292 to 155. Winning twenty-eight states in all, McKinley swept the North again, added all the Plains states to his list, and captured Wyoming, Utah, Washington, Oregon, and California in the West. Again he cracked the South, taking the Border States of Delaware, Maryland, and West Virginia. Bryan won only thirteen southern states plus the silver states of Montana, Colorado, Idaho, and Nevada. Disfranchisement continued to diminish African American voting in the Deep South; in South Carolina, Florida, Georgia, Mississippi, and Louisiana, turnout fell below 30 percent. In the congressional elections, the Republicans made gains over 1898 and would have substantial majorities in the new House and Senate.

With four overwhelming victories since 1894, the Republicans clearly established themselves as the nation's majority party, a position they would not relinquish until the economic disaster of 1929 worked another major realignment in American politics. The American people had selected William McKinley to lead them into the twentieth century. As the apostle of nationalism and the political beneficiary of prosperity, McKinley decisively turned the nation away from the old Civil War party system, although the idiom of race and section remained dominant in the South, where the Democrats maintained their grip for decades. In the future, economics and foreign affairs would take center stage in national politics.

McKinley also operated as a transitional figure in the conduct of the government. As a congressman, he had watched Benjamin Harrison's judicious lobbying of Congress, his use of the press, and his willingness to travel and take the case for his policies to the people. After the disastrous second Cleveland administration, McKinley picked up where Harrison had left off and proved highly effective in making the presidency the center of the American government. He used his direct appeals to the public to build a power base independent of his constitutionally defined relationship with Congress. On the eve of McKinley's second inauguration, an observer wrote, "The pivot upon which we revolve as a nation is no longer the Capitol, where the people's representatives assemble, but the White House, where one man sits in almost supreme power."[24]

McKinley was denied the opportunity to build on his record in his second term. In September 1901 he visited the Pan-American Exposition in Buffalo, New York, where he urged public support for trade reciprocity, for aid to rebuild the merchant marine, and for American construction of a ship canal through Central America. The next day, while shaking hands in a receiving line, the president was shot by an anarchist named Leon Czolgosz. McKinley died on September 14, 1901, and was succeeded by Theodore Roosevelt. Although Czolgosz was emotionally disturbed and harbored nebulous political notions, his suspicion of all government led him to remove one of the nation's foremost advocates of activist government. But as a political act, the assassination backfired, for it raised to the presidency a man whose vision of government's role evolved even beyond McKinley's.

A robust and vigorous leader, Theodore Roosevelt quickly concluded that rapidly changing circumstances required the national government to move beyond such standard concerns as taxation, the currency, and defense, and to give greater attention to business regulation, conservation, and other issues affecting citizens' well-being. Historically, Americans believed that state and local governments were the proper venues to deal with such matters as working conditions, the environment, education, and health, and in this new period, soon to be labeled the Progressive Era, these entities were beginning to exercise more responsible government. But the unwillingness or inability of states to act generated new pressures for the federal government to tackle these vital questions, and Progressivism moved to the national level.

In the last three decades of the nineteenth century, the political struggles of the Gilded Age had laid the groundwork for this transformation and the emergence of the modern American polity. In the great debates over civil rights and economic policy that dominated the three decades after the Civil War, the underlying question concerned what role the national government should play in the society. In the late 1860s and early 1870s, nationally oriented Republicans, whose first great achievement had been the preservation of the nation itself, invoked the power of the federal government to rework social and political arrangements in the South and to guarantee fundamental rights to the freed slaves and their descendants. In the name of states' rights, Democrats strenuously resisted those efforts, and in the service of white supremacy, southerners proved willing to go to any length to overturn reforms and hold African Americans in second-class citizenship. With the passage of time, northerners became increasingly less willing to follow the Republicans' charge, the party's commitment to egalitarian ideals waned, and the experiment of Reconstruction ended in failure.

Even before that outcome, however, politicians' attention had begun to turn away from sectional issues to economic questions. The need to accommodate wartime fiscal and monetary restructuring to peacetime needs, coupled with the imperatives of a burgeoning industrialization, made it inevitable that issues related to the economy would move to the forefront. As one Republican national chairman put it, "economic issues, every one of them affecting the comfort and welfare of every home, had superseded the war issues," and each party "had to show to every family, to every business interest, to every one of the different classes of workingmen, and to women as well as men, its superiority in protecting and advancing their interests."[25]

In addressing those new issues, nationally oriented Republicans such as James G. Blaine, John Sherman, Benjamin Harrison, and William McKinley envisioned an expansive role for the federal government in managing the economy to further the nation's development. Unlike the Cleveland Democrats, still imbued with the small-government notions of Jefferson and Jackson, these Republicans had come to accept the notion that government was more than a negative force, that it could do something to stimulate the country's growth and thereby improve the lot of the people. They argued that such policies as a protective tariff, reciprocity, a stable currency, and government subsidies served not merely individual interests but the national interest. And in pressing the argument for government action, they not only charted a course for their own time; they also set the stage for the great contest in the Progressive Era over the duty and function of government in a modern society. In the debate between Progressives and conservatives, Theodore Roosevelt, Woodrow Wilson, and other new leaders embraced the national emphasis and energetic impulses that had been the hallmark of Gilded Age Republicans. Ultimately, however, while building on that vision, the Progressives went beyond it. They carried government activism beyond the level of trickle-down macroeconomics to a new, more direct concern for the welfare of citizens in the evolving economic and social order of the twentieth century.

NOTES

SUGGESTIONS FOR FURTHER READING

INDEX

Notes

Abbreviations

BH-Home   Benjamin Harrison Papers, Benjamin Harrison Home, Indianapolis

BH-LC   Benjamin Harrison Papers, Library of Congress

CG   *Congressional Globe*

CR   *Congressional Record*

EBW-LC   Elihu B. Washburne Papers, Library of Congress

GC-LC   Grover Cleveland Papers, Library of Congress

H-BP   *Hand-Book of Politics* (comp. Edward McPherson; Washington, D.C.: various publishers, 1872–94; cited by year and page number)

JAGD   *The Diary of James A. Garfield* (comp. Harry James Brown and Frederick D. Williams; East Lansing: Michigan State University Press, 1967–81)

JCS-LC   John Coit Spooner Papers, Library of Congress

JS-LC   John Sherman Papers, Library of Congress

JSC-LC   James S. Clarkson Papers, Library of Congress

JSM-LC   Justin S. Morrill Papers, Library of Congress

LC   Library of Congress

LGC   *Letters of Grover Cleveland: 1850–1908* (ed. Allan Nevins; Boston: Houghton Mifflin, 1933)

M & P   *Messages and Papers of the Presidents* (comp. James D. Richardson; Washington, D.C.: Bureau of National Literature and Art, 1903)

NPP   *National Party Platforms, 1840–1972* (comp. Donald Bruce Johnson and Kirk H. Porter; Urbana: University of Illinois Press, 1975)

NYH   *New York Herald*

NYT   *The New York Times*

NYTr   *New York Tribune*

PUSG   *The Papers of Ulysses S. Grant* (ed. John Y. Simon; Carbondale: Southern Illinois University Press, 1967–)

RBHDL	*Diary and Letters of Rutherford Birchard Hayes* (ed. Charles Richard Williams; Columbus: Ohio State Archaeological and Historical Society, 1922–26)
SBH	*Speeches of Benjamin Harrison* (comp. Charles Hedges; New York: United States Book Company, 1892)
SJR-HSP	Samuel J. Randall Papers, Historical Society of Pennsylvania, Philadelphia
WR-LC	Reid Family Papers, Library of Congress

Preface

1. Theodore Roosevelt, "The Manly Virtues and Practical Politics," *Forum* 17 (July 1894): 552.

Introduction

1. James S. Clarkson, draft of speech "Delivered at Louisville KY as Pres[iden]t of Nat[iona]l League of Clubs at Annual Meeting" [1893], JSC-LC.

1. General in the White House

1. *PUSG*, 18:292.
2. James G. Blaine, *Twenty Years of Congress* (Norwich, Conn.: Henry Bill, 1884, 1886), 2:412.
3. *NPP*, 39.
4. Eric Foner, *Reconstruction: America's Unfinished Revolution, 1863–1877* (New York: Harper & Row, 1988), 340; James D. McCabe, *The Life and Public Service of Horatio Seymour* (New York: United States Publishing Co., 1868), 226; Edward McPherson, *Political History of the United States of America During the Period of Reconstruction* (Washington, D.C.: Philp & Solomons, 1871), 368, 381.
5. *PUSG*, 18:264.
6. *CG*, 40–3, appx., 99.
7. *PUSG*, 18:295n; *M & P*, 7:6.
8. *M & P*, 7:7.
9. *Letters of Henry Adams (1858–1891)*, ed. Worthington Chauncey Ford (Boston: Houghton Mifflin, 1930), 156.
10. *PUSG*, 19:244.
11. *M & P*, 7:29.
12. *CG*, 41–2, appx., 51; Benjamin F. Butler, *Public Expenditures of Grant's Administration* (Washington, D.C.: Congressional Globe Office, 1870), 15.
13. Adam Badeau to J.C.B. Davis, June 23, 1870, J. C. Bancroft Davis Papers, LC.
14. *CG*, 41–2, 3608, 3609; *PUSG*, 20:91.

15. Henry Wilson to Hamilton Fish, October 31, 1870, Hamilton Fish Papers, LC.
16. *M & P*, 7:109.
17. *CG*, 42–1, 690.
18. *The Gilded Age Letters of E. L. Godkin*, ed. William M. Armstrong (Albany: State University of New York Press, 1974), 186–87.
19. *NPP*, 44.
20. *Republicanism vs. Grantism . . . Speech of Hon. Charles Sumner, of Massachusetts, Delivered in the Senate of the United States, May 31, 1872* (Washington, D.C.: F. & J. Rives & Geo. A. Bailey, 1872), 7, 17.
21. *H-BP*, 1872, 209; Edwards Pierrepont, *Speech of the Hon. Edwards Pierrepont, Delivered Before the Republican Mass Meeting, at Wilgus Hall, Ithica, N.Y., October 11th, 1872* (New York: Evening Post Steam Presses, 1872), 14.
22. *NYT*, August 12, September 25, 1872; B. Gratz Brown, *Speech of Gov. B. Gratz Brown, of Missouri, Delivered in the Academy of Music, Indianapolis, Ind., Wednesday Evening, Sept. 11, 1872* (Indianapolis: Indianapolis Sentinel, 1872), 6; Charles Sumner, *Letter to Colored Citizens by Hon. Charles Sumner, July 29, 1872* (Washington, D.C.: F. & J. Rives & Geo. A. Bailey, 1872), 6, 8.
23. *M & P*, 7:244, 269; *NYTr*, April 23, 1874. Grant erred in citing a $100 million increase; it was $90 million. *PUSG*, 25:75n.

2. Hayes: Uncertain Triumph

1. Marshall Jewell to Elihu Washburne, April 23, 1875, EBW-LC.
2. *M & P*, 7:205, 255, 301.
3. JAGD, 3:6; *PUSG*, 26:135n.
4. Charles Richard Williams, *The Life of Rutherford Birchard Hayes* (Columbus: Ohio State Archaeological and Historical Society, 1928), 1:393; RBHDL, 3:283, 286.
5. *H-BP* (1876), 155–56, 228.
6. Edwards Pierrepont to Elihu Washburne, November 3, 1875, EBW-LC; B. H. Bristow to J. K. Gant, December 2, 1875, Benjamin H. Bristow Papers, LC; JAGD, 3:176.
7. JAGD, 3:204.
8. Julia B. Foraker, *I Would Live It Again: Memories of a Vivid Life* (New York: Harper & Brothers, 1932), 132.
9. Blaine, *Twenty Years of Congress*, 2:554; John W. Forney to Elihu Washburne, February 5, 1876, EBW-LC.
10. *PUSG*, 27:45n.
11. R. R. Hitt to O. P. Morton, April 21, 1876, R. R. Hitt Papers, LC.
12. *CR*, 44-1, 3604.
13. *Speeches, Correspondence and Political Papers of Carl Schurz*, ed. Frederic Bancroft (New York: G. P. Putnam's Sons, 1913), 3:245.

14. *Official Proceedings of the National Republican Conventions of 1868, 1872, 1876, and 1880* (Minneapolis: Charles W. Johnson, 1903), 293, 296, 299.
15. *NPP*, 53–55.
16. Samuel J. Tilden to Abram S. Hewitt, July 15, 1876, Samuel J. Tilden Papers, New York Public Library; Michael F. Holt, *By One Vote: The Disputed Presidential Election of 1876* (Lawrence: University Press of Kansas, 2008), 132; *NPP*, 49–51.
17. *H-BP* (1876), 212–13.
18. Ibid., 217–22.
19. *Letters and Literary Memorials of Samuel J. Tilden*, ed. John Bigelow (New York: Harper and Brothers, 1908), 2:470; Holt, *By One Vote*, 138.
20. Senate Executive Document No. 85, 44th Cong., 1st sess., 5; *CR*, 44-1, 5280; Edwards Pierrepont to Elihu Washburne, October 14, 1876, EBW-LC; Hayes to James A. Garfield, August 5, 1876, James A. Garfield Papers, LC.
21. Carl Schurz, *To Business Men. Address by Hon. Carl Schurz, Before the Union League Club, of New York, Saturday Evening, October 21, 1876* (New York: Republican National Committee, 1876), 7; Hayes to Murat Halstead, October 14, 1876, Murat Halstead Papers, Cincinnati Historical Society; RBHDL, 3:373.
22. W. E. Stevens to William E. Chandler, August 24, 1877, William E. Chandler Papers, New Hampshire Historical Society, Concord.
23. R. B. Hayes to C. W. Goddard, September 26, 1878, Rutherford B. Hayes Papers, Rutherford B. Hayes Presidential Center, Fremont, Ohio.
24. RBHDL, 3:509; JAGD, 4:143–44.
25. George C. Gorham to William E. Chandler, October 16, 1878, William E. Chandler Papers, LC; RBHDL, 3:510.
26. *M & P*, 7:531; *Garfield-Hinsdale Letters: Correspondence Between James Abram Garfield and Burke Aaron Hinsdale*, ed. Mary L. Hinsdale (Ann Arbor: University of Michigan Press, 1949), 416.

3. "Fold Up the Bloody Shirt"

1. George S. Boutwell, "General Grant and a Third Term," *North American Review* 130 (April 1880): 384; D. W. Voyles to Walter Q. Gresham, November 3, 1879, Noble C. Butler Papers, Indiana Historical Society, Indianapolis.
2. *NPP*, 62.
3. *NPP*, 60–62.
4. *NPP*, 56–57; *Boston Evening Transcript*, July 1, 1880.
5. RBHDL, 3:615; *The Republican Campaign Textbook for 1880* (Washington, D.C.: Republican Congressional Committee, 1880).
6. *H-BP* (1880), 210B–210C.
7. William C. Hudson, *Random Recollections of an Old Political Reporter* (New York: Cuples & Long, 1911), 112.

8. *Paterson Guardian* (New Jersey) quoted in *Cincinnati Gazette*, October 11, 1880; *NYTr*, October 19, 1880.

9. James A. Garfield to John Sherman, November 4, 1880, JS-LC.

10. Thomas C. Reeves, *Gentleman Boss: The Life of Chester Alan Arthur* (New York: Knopf, 1975), 237.

11. *M & P*, 8:121–22; *CR*, 47-1, 6305.

12. *M & P*, 8:49.

13. *M & P*, 8:145–46.

14. *M & P*, 8:135–36; *Annual Report of the Secretary of the Treasury . . . 1882* (Washington, D.C.: Government Printing Office, 1882), xxxiii.

15. Joseph Wharton to Justin Morrill, February 1, 1883, JSM-LC.

16. Fred P. Fox to John Sherman, September 3, 1883; Sherman to H. C. Jones, August 8, 1883; D. Harpster to Sherman, October 25, 1883, JS-LC.

17. Blaine, *Twenty Years of Congress*, 1:200.

18. H. Wayne Morgan, *William McKinley and His America* (Kent, Ohio: Kent State University Press, 2003), 61; *NPP*, 72–74.

19. Hans L. Trefousse, *Carl Schurz* (Knoxville: University of Tennessee Press, 1982), 261.

20. *Official Proceedings of the National Democratic Convention, Held in Chicago, Ill., July 8th, 9th, 10th, and 11th, 1884* (New York: Douglas Taylor, 1884), 176.

21. *NPP*, 65–68.

22. *Address of the National Conference of Republicans and Independents, New York, 1884* (Boston: Republican and Independent Headquarters, 1884).

23. *Buffalo Evening Telegraph*, July 21, 1884.

24. Grover Cleveland, *The Writings and Speeches of Grover Cleveland*, ed. George F. Parker (New York: Cassell, 1892), 301, 302.

25. T. B. Boyd, *The Blaine and Logan Campaign of 1884* (Chicago: J. L. Reagan, 1884), 44, 104.

26. Ibid., 146.

27. Ibid., 189, 191; *New York World*, October 30, 1884.

28. Boyd, *Blaine and Logan Campaign*, 226.

29. *LGC*, 48.

4. Grover Cleveland: The Last Jacksonian

1. *Speeches, Correspondence and Political Papers of Carl Schurz*, 4:351.

2. Charles W. Calhoun, *Minority Victory: Gilded Age Politics and the Front Porch Campaign of 1888* (Lawrence: University Press of Kansas, 2008), 33; *CR*, 49-1, 2790–97.

3. *Speeches, Correspondence and Political Papers of Carl Schurz*, 4:436; *LGC*, 177.

4. *LGC*, 57.

5. *M & P*, 8:300.

6. *M & P*, 8:302.

7. *M & P*, 8:555.
8. *M & P*, 8:557.
9. Allan Nevins, *Grover Cleveland: A Study in Courage* (New York: Dodd, Mead, 1932), 333; J. B. Foraker, "The Return of the Republican Party," *Forum* 3 (August 1887): 545; "Many Democrats" to Grover Cleveland, June 17, 1887, GC-LC.
10. John C. Spooner to Frank Avery, January 7, 1888, JCS-LC.
11. *M & P*, 8:185, 526.
12. *M & P*, 8:509; George Hoadly to Grover Cleveland, November 22, 1887, GC-LC.
13. *M & P*, 8:580–91.
14. *NYTr*, December 8, 1887.
15. J. W. Cooper to Samuel J. Randall, December 8, 1887, SJR-HSP; *NYH*, December 7, 1887; Grover Cleveland to Thomas F. Bayard, December 18, 1887, Thomas F. Bayard Papers, LC.
16. John W. Davis to Grover Cleveland, April 6, 1888, GC-LC.
17. *NPP*, 77; *NYT*, June 7, 1888.
18. Grover Cleveland, draft of platform, dated (in another's hand) May 31, 1888, GC-LC; *NPP*, 77.
19. *NYTr*, February 13, 1888; James G. Blaine to Whitelaw Reid, October 11, 1887, WR-LC.
20. Blaine to Stephen B. Elkins, March 1, 1888, Stephen B. Elkins Papers, West Virginia University Library, Morgantown.
21. *NPP*, 79–82.
22. *H-BP* (1890), 31, 33; Samuel Randall to Calvin Brice, October 10, 1888, SJR-HSP.
23. *NYH*, September 11, 1888; *H-BP* (1890), 27.
24. Benjamin Harrison to Whitelaw Reid, September 27, 1888, WR-LC; *SBH*, 162–63.
25. John W. Plummer to Benjamin Harrison, August 21, 1888, with news clipping, BH-LC; *NYH*, October 28, 1888.
26. *Indianapolis Journal*, October 8, 1888; *Indianapolis Sentinel*, October 31, 1888.
27. *The Correspondence Between Benjamin Harrison and James G. Blaine, 1882–1893*, ed. Albert T. Volwiler (Philadelphia: American Philosophical Society, 1940), 41.

5. Harrison, Cleveland, and the Purposes of Power

1. *M & P*, 8:773–78.
2. *M & P*, 9:5–14.
3. Thomas B. Reed, "Rules of the House of Representatives," *Century Magazine* 37 (March, 1989): 795.

4. L. T. Michener to E. W. Halford, November 26, 1889, BH-LC.

5. Benjamin Harrison to Caroline Harrison, July 13, 1890, BH-Home.

6. *M & P*, 9:56.

7. Frederick Douglass to George F. Hoar, September 2, 1890, George F. Hoar Papers, Massachusetts Historical Society, Boston.

8. R. Hal Williams, *Years of Decision: American Politics in the 1890s* (New York: John Wiley & Sons, 1978), 41; *SBH*, 263.

9. L. T. Michener to E. W. Halford, November 8, 1890, Benjamin Harrison to Howard Cale, November 17, 1890, Harrison to R. S. Taylor, November 29, 1890, BH-LC.

10. John G. Carlisle, "The Recent Election," *North American Review* 151 (December 1890): 642; *LGC*, 236.

11. *CR*, 51-2: 245, 873; J. C. Spooner to G. L. Chapin, March 8, 1891, JCS-LC.

12. Henry Cabot Lodge to Anna Cabot Lodge, March 8, 1891, Henry Cabot Lodge Papers, Massachusetts Historical Society, Boston; *NYTr*, March 17, 1891; *Indianapolis Journal*, March 5, 1891.

13. *NPP*, 93–95.

14. *Official Proceedings of the National Democratic Convention, Held in Chicago, Ill., June 21st, 22nd, and 23rd, 1892* (Chicago: Cameron, Amberg & Co., 1892), 77, 79, 82; Mark D. Hirsch, *William C. Whitney: Modern Warwick* (New York: Dodd, Mead, 1948), 398.

15. *Official Proceedings of the National Democratic Convention . . . 1892*, 76.

16. *H-BP* (1892), 269–71.

17. *NYT*, July 21, 1892.

18. *H-BP* (1894), 35, 36.

19. Ibid., 24, 25, 27, 30.

20. Ibid., 28; *The Republican Campaign Text-book for 1892* (New York: Brodix Publishing, 1892), 198–99.

21. *New York Sun*, June 24, July 8, 24, 1892; *NYT*, July 14, 19, 1892.

22. H. Wayne Morgan, *From Hayes to McKinley: National Party Politics, 1877–1896* (Syracuse, N.Y.: Syracuse University Press, 1969), 431.

23. Williams, *Years of Decision*, 64.

24. Charles H. Aldrich to E. W. Halford, December 4, 1892, BH-LC.

25. *Indianapolis Journal*, December 31, 1892; *M & P*, 9:310, 332.

26. *M & P*, 9:389, 390, 392.

27. *M & P*, 9:402.

28. George Edmunds to Justin Morrill, September 16, 1893, JSM-LC.

29. *M & P*, 9:488; *NYT*, April 6, 1894.

30. *LGC*, 355.

31. *Democratic Campaign Book* (Washington, D.C.: Hartman & Cadick, 1894), 8; Robert P. Porter, *Life of William McKinley, Soldier, Lawyer, Statesman* (Cleveland: N. G. Hamilton, 1896), 234.

6. The Emerging Republican Majority

1. William A. Robinson, *Thomas B. Reed: Parliamentarian* (New York: Dodd, Mead, 1930), 327.

2. *Official Proceedings of the Eleventh Republican National Convention Held in the City of St. Louis, Mo., June 16, 17 and 18, 1896* (Minneapolis: C. W. Johnson, 1896), 83, 84.

3. *Official Proceedings of the Democratic National Convention Held in Chicago, Ill., July 7th, 8th, 9th, 10th, and 11th, 1896* (Logansport, Ind.: Wilson, Humphreys, 1896), 193, 195, 196, 198, 208, 247, 249.

4. Ibid., 192, 197, 234, 241, 252.

5. Ibid., 269.

6. *LGC*, 446, 456.

7. John Hay to Whitelaw Reid, August 31, 1896, WR-LC; Williams, *Years of Decision*, 119–22.

8. *Official Proceedings of the Republican National Convention . . . 1896*, 159; *McKinley's Speeches in August*, comp. Joseph P. Smith (n.p.: Republican National Committee, 1896), 90–92.

9. *M & P*, 10:12–14.

10. *M & P*, 10:15, 18; *Speeches and Addresses of William McKinley from March 1, 1897 to May 30, 1900* (New York: Doubleday & McClure, 1900), 159, 177, 178.

11. *M & P*, 10:16–17.

12. *Appletons' Annual Cyclopaedia and Register of Important Events of the Year 1897* (New York: D. Appleton, 1898), 542.

13. Ibid., 652.

14. William Roscoe Thayer, *The Life and Letters of John Hay* (Boston: Houghton Mifflin, 1915), 2:337.

15. *Speeches and Addresses of William McKinley from March 1, 1897 to May 30, 1900*, 85, 87, 109, 114, 141, 145.

16. *Appletons' Annual Cyclopaedia and Register of Important Events of the Year 1898* (New York: D. Appleton, 1899), 498, 499; *NYT*, June 15, 1898; Benjamin Harrison to R. S. Taylor, October 19, 1898, BH-Home.

17. Lewis L. Gould, *The Presidency of William McKinley* (Lawrence: Regents Press of Kansas, 1980), 137.

18. William Jennings Bryan, *Republic or Empire? The Philippine Question* (Chicago: Independence Company, 1899), 696.

19. *Appletons' Annual Cyclopaedia and Register of Important Events of the Year 1899* (New York: D. Appleton, 1900), 680.

20. *NYT*, October 22, 1899; *Speeches and Addresses of McKinley*, 339, 340, 342.

21. *NPP*, 122–24.

22. *NPP*, 113, 114, 122.

23. *Official Proceedings of the Twelfth Republican National Convention Held in*

the City of Philadelphia, June 19, 20, 21, 1900 (Philadelphia: Dunlap Printing, 1900), 158, 161, 173.

24. Henry Litchfield West, "The Growing Powers of the President," *Forum* 31 (March 1901): 23–24.

25. James S. Clarkson to Welker Given, August 13, 1894, JSC-LC.

Suggestions for Further Reading

Bensel, Richard Franklin. *The Political Economy of American Industrialization, 1877–1900*. Cambridge: Cambridge University Press, 2000.

Calhoun, Charles W. *Conceiving a New Republic: The Republican Party and the Southern Question, 1869–1900*. Lawrence: University Press of Kansas, 2006.

———. *Minority Victory: Gilded Age Politics and the Front Porch Campaign of 1888*. Lawrence: University Press of Kansas, 2008

———, ed. *The Gilded Age: Perspectives on the Origins of Modern America*. Lanham, Md.: Rowman & Littlefield, 2007.

Cherny, Robert W. *American Politics in the Gilded Age, 1868–1900*. Wheeling, Ill.: Harlan Davidson, 1997.

Doenecke, Justus D. *The Presidencies of James A. Garfield & Chester A. Arthur*. Lawrence: Regents Press of Kansas, 1981.

Edwards, Rebecca. *Angels in the Machinery: Gender in American Party Politics from the Civil War to the Progressive Era*. New York: Oxford University Press, 1997.

Gould, Lewis L. *The Presidency of William McKinley*. Lawrence: Regents Press of Kansas, 1980.

Holt, Michael F. *By One Vote: The Disputed Presidential Election of 1876*. Lawrence: University Press of Kansas, 2008.

Hoogenboom, Ari. *The Presidency of Rutherford B. Hayes*. Lawrence: University Press of Kansas, 1988.

Jensen, Richard. *The Winning of the Midwest: Social and Political Conflict, 1888–1896*. Chicago: University of Chicago Press, 1971.

Josephson, Matthew. *The Politicos, 1865–1896*. New York: Harcourt, Brace, 1938.

Kazin, Michael. *A Godly Hero: The Life of William Jennings Bryan*. New York: Knopf, 2006.

Marcus, Robert D. *Grand Old Party: Political Structure in the Gilded Age, 1880–1896*. New York: Oxford University Press, 1971.

McGerr, Michael E. *The Decline of Popular Politics: The American North, 1865–1928*. New York: Oxford University Press, 1986.

McGrath, Robert C. *American Populism: A Social History, 1877–1898*. New York: Farrar, Straus and Giroux, 1992.

Morgan, H. Wayne. *From Hayes to McKinley: National Party Politics, 1877–1896*. Syracuse, N.Y.: Syracuse University Press, 1969.

Nevins, Allan. *Grover Cleveland: A Study in Courage*. New York: Dodd, Mead, 1932.

Peskin, Allan. *Garfield*. Kent, Ohio: Kent State University Press, 1999.

Reeves, Thomas C. *Gentleman Boss: The Life of Chester Alan Arthur*. New York: Knopf, 1975.

Simpson, Brooks D. *The Reconstruction Presidents*. Lawrence: University Press of Kansas, 1998.

Sproat, John G. *"The Best Men": Liberal Reformers in the Gilded Age*. New York: Oxford University Press, 1968.

Summers, Mark Wahlgren. *Party Games: Getting, Keeping, and Using Power in Gilded Age Politics*. Chapel Hill: University of North Carolina Press, 2004.

Unger, Irwin. *The Greenback Era: A Social and Political History of American Finance, 1865–1879*. Princeton, N.J.: Princeton University Press, 1964.

Welch, Richard E., Jr. *The Presidencies of Grover Cleveland*. Lawrence: University Press of Kansas, 1988.

Williams, R. Hal. *Realigning America: McKinley, Bryan, and the Remarkable Election of 1896*. Lawrence: University Press of Kansas, 2010.

———. *Years of Decision: American Politics in the 1890s*. New York: John Wiley & Sons, 1978.

INDEX

Page numbers in *italics* refer to illustrations.

New York Tribune, 141
New York World, 94
North, 39, 43, 45, 55, 62, 64, 101, 179;
    election of 1880 and, 71; election of
    1884 and, 94, 95; election of 1896 and,
    164; South's reconciliation with, 100,
    102, 167, 173
North Carolina, 30, 121, 143, 164, 167
North Dakota, 145, 164
Northeast, 6, 144, 150, 161, 164, 178

Ohio, 43–45, 62, 81, 105, 111, 176;
    election of 1894 in, 149; election of
    1897 in, 170, 171
Ohio Idea, 14
Oregon, 55, 75, 110, 145, 180

Pan-American Conference, 136
Pan-American Exposition, 181
Panic of 1873, 34, *35*
Panic of 1893, 146–49
Paris Peace Conference (1898), 173–75
patronage, 7, 53; Arthur and, 76, 78;
    Cleveland and, 88, 98–99, 136, 139,
    148; Garfield and, 75; Grant and,
    20–21, 26, 28–30; Harrison and, 136;
    Hayes and, 52, 59, 61, 68; McKinley
    and, 175
Pendleton, George H., 14
Pendleton Civil Service Act (1883), 7, 79,
    98
Pennsylvania, 45, 62, 71, 108, 140–41, 149
Pension Bureau, U.S., 101
Philadelphia and Reading Railroad, 147
Philippines, 172, 174–75, 176, 178, 179
Pierrepont, Edwards, 43, 45, 54
Platt, Thomas C., 84, 137
political clubs, 8
polygamy, 70, 85
Populists (People's Party), 8, 132, 147,
    154, 174; election of 1892 and, 139–40,
    142–45; election of 1896 and, 159, 161,
    163, 165; middle-of-the-road vs.
    fusionists, 161

Post Office, U.S., 20, 24, 99, 135, 139, 153
Progressive Era, 181–83
prohibition, 81
Prohibition Party, 8, 89
prosperity, 84, 93, 107, 141, 145, 148, 170;
    McKinley and, 163, 164, 165, 173, 179;
    return of, 70, 72, 77, 165, 170, 173, 176,
    178, 179
Protestants, 45, 93
Public Credit Act (1869), 21
public works, 24–25, 152, 161
Puck, *104*, *128*
Puerto Rico, 172, 175
Pullman Palace Car Company, 153

Quay, Matthew, 137

race question, x, 4, 5, 6, 69, 111, 180;
    election of 1892 and, 143, 144; Hayes
    and, 59; voting rights and, *see* blacks,
    voting rights of
racism, 15, 33
Radical Republicans, 12, 15, 19
railroads, 34, 49, 61, 89; closing of, 147;
    government ownership of, 140, 161;
    regulation of, 85, 103; strikes and, 141,
    153
Randall, Samuel J., 71, 87, 105, 108, 116
Rawlins, John A., 19
recession, 13–14
reciprocity agreements, 126, 136, 158,
    163, 165, 167, 169, 179
Reconstruction, 4, 5, 11–15, 30, 64, 119,
    143; attack on legal vestiges of, 150;
    demise of, 6, 130, 182; election of 1868
    and, 11, 14, 15; election of 1872 and,
    32, 33; Grant and, 17, 28, 32, 39;
    Hancock and, 71; Hayes and, 54, 60;
    management problems and, 36
Reconstruction Amendments, 54, 59
Reed, Thomas B., 125, 130, 132, 144,
    154, 158
reform, 83; election of 1876 and, 46,
    49–53; *see also* civil service reform